TRAVELLING ACROSS SOUTH AFRICAN BORDERS

- AN ESSENTIAL GUIDE -

Dennis J Mkhulisi

ISBN: 978-0-620-81015-9
Published by: www.myebook.co.za
Publication date: September 2018
Printed by: Amazon

ABOUT THE AUTHOR

Dennis Mkhulisi is a semi-retired South African born medical practitioner and entrepreneur. He has been blessed to travel extensively outside the South African borders. He also has a passion for nature photography.

CONTENTS

FOREWORD

Travellers are-by nature-driven. They are driven by the passion to see unfamiliar places, feel the vibe of a different music genre, explore new business opportunities and to meet people of a different cultural background. Zouk music in Maputo and Maskandi music in KwaZulu-Natal are distinct music genres that easily come to mind. Vast coal deposits exist in the south eastern border of Botswana (with South Africa) as well as in the central provinces of Tete and Gaza in Mozambique). SASOL-a South African petrochemical conglomerate-is already tapping gas deposits off the coast of Qualimane (Mozambique).

The mining of bauxite contributes nearly 50% to the Mozambican fiscus. Its northern and north eastern border of Mozambican border (with Malawi) harbours vast bauxite deposits too. Deep sea fishing off the Mozambican coast has been a favourite pastime for South African and their international guests. Offshore Namibian crude oil deposits await exploration. Diamond mining in that country has been a solid contributor to her fiscus for decades. Sossuvlei dunes are of legendary beauty. Zimbabwe has the world's largest platinum reserves! Impala platinum's mining activities are arguably the largest contributor to Zimbabwe's fiscus. The eastern highlands of Zimbabwe-with their clear spring water spruits-are a tourist's gem awaiting YOUR visit!!

To explore all these emotions one has to enter a country of interest by road. One's passport, driver's licence, "enough" cash, medical/travel insurance often guarantees one entry into one's destination. Commonly, accommodation for the first night at least would have been booked in advance. For the intrepid traveller who has read several travel guides, "bargain" deals may be found on arrival. This may add to one's miles to travel as some hotels may be fully booked. So far so good..?

That rented/owned car may suffer an electrical fault and stall hopefully along the main freeway. Who do you call? What do you do next when you get NO response from that emergency number you've called? Okay, someone responds immediately and promises to send someone "shortly". That someone rocks up an hour later, has a cursory look at the engine compartment, tinkers a bit and then tells you an auto-electrician is need to sort out your car's problem. What next?

You arrive at the border post and money changers offer you the "best rate"...

Border controls done, you drive leisurely AND carefully in a new country's highway to the nearest town/main city and a goat/cow suddenly appears on the edge of the road (to try and cross over to the sweeter grass), you swerve to avoid it and land up in a ditch on the other side of the road. (Let's just say luck is on your side, there's no car driving in the opposite direction at that moment). Dazed and shaken, you ring the supplied emergency number and the response is "...the number you've just dialled does not exist..!" Who do you call next?

What about "wrongful" arrest and incarceration in a foreign country? Yes, you do have rights! So, you humbly ask the officer to get you a lawyer or, at least, put you through to your country's embassy and he just gawks at you... What if your country has no embassy nor has it accredited any other embassy (to handle her nationals' needs)?

Yes, you do have travel insurance jampacked with millions of dollars of evacuation and medical insurance, but-with all your belongings locked away-what will you do?

You are a global business mogul who yearns to explore for coal, platinum in a foreign country. Your pilot is ready to point your private jet's noise to Eutopia country but its airport does not meet international standards. Do you fly there regardless?

Worse still, fatalities sadly do occur whilst people are in transit. How do your next of kin locate and repatriate your mortal remains?

These and other are pertinent and therefore have to be planned for IN ADVANCE. This guide serves to unravel many, if not all, often neglected issues when one travels. Further, we seek to update our readers of changes to the information provided herein-as soon as it becomes available.

Through our website we will provide important and urgent alerts, to help YOU avoid potentially dangerous areas. Such dangers may be posed by freak natural disasters, political unrest or disease outbreaks.

INTRODUCTION

South Africa, the southernmost country in Africa, is the largest economy in Africa. It's the only African member of globally recognized and quoted "emerging economies" colloquially called BRICS countries (Brazil, Russia, India, China and South Africa). Its natural resources are traded globally. It home to the largest stock exchange (by size and value) in Africa. It's a world class conference venue with a highly advanced banking system. Several global banking brands are represented here.

It has-over the years-hosted several successful sporting events such as the annual Nedbank golf challenge at Sun City, the world renowned annual Comrades marathon, the rugby (1995) and the soccer (2010) world cups. South Africa has recently been added in the Formula One car racing calendar with effect from 2012. The KYALAMI race track has been in existence for more than a decade.

It is a stable democracy with an excellent infrastructure. The top three airports in Africa are in South Africa, namely, OR TAMBO International, King Shaka International and Cape Town International airports-as rated by SKYTRAX. For the traveller (for leisure or for business) South Africa offers reliable cutting edge internet broadband connectivity countrywide.

These pillars of the economy have ensured a sustainable interest in South Africa by tourists and business travellers from all over the world, including heads of global conglomerates wishing to invest in the African diaspora. Global humanitarian organizations are active in Africa due to several catastrophies, for instance, the devastating floods in Mozambique, the protracted civil wars in Angola, Zaire (now called the Democratic Republic of the Congo) and Zimbabwe.

Foreign guests (business persons and humanitarian functionaries) very often make South Africa their initial port of call whereafter-with the assistance of skilled South African nationals-they plan their entry into the rest of the African continent. SA Tourism and Airports Company of South Africa, amongst others-project an exponential increase in inbound tourists to South Africa-either by air or by road.

It's our primary aim to present all necessary information in one publication to ease passage of foreign guests through South Africa's borders by road. It is through these borders that travellers pay for essentially free services or get delayed for a long time because of incomplete required documents. Further, not all services that are generally available in South Africa are easily accessible in neighbouring countries.

Very few countries of the world have embassies/high commissioners in countries neighbouring South Africa. In these instances needs of their compatriots are handling by their South African offices/embassies.

CHAPTER ONE

BORDER ACCESS CONTROL

SA BORDER WITH BOTSWANA

In this section we will only deal with easily accessible routes from either Pretoria, Johannesburg or Cape Town. From Pretoria the most convenient route is to head for Brits on the N4 highway, then Rustenburg, Groot Marico and then Zeerust. From there the Pioneer Gate-Skilpadshek/ Gate border post [25°27'56"S-25°71'38"E] will be reached in less than an hour's leisurely drive.

Opening times are: 06h00 – 24h00
Telephone: +27-18-366 0011

From Johannesburg two options are available, namely, heading for Brits on the R511national road to join the N4 highway and follow the previous route or head for Krugersdorp on the N14 highway past Ventersdorp. At Coligny [26°20'30"S-26°18'19"E] branch off to Lichtenburg. Here you again you have to choices, namely heading past Bakerville on the R505 national road to Zeerust [25°32'42"S-26°04'45"E] or heading for Lichtenburg and then on to

Mahikeng/Mafikeng along the R503 to enter Botswana along N18 highway at Ramatlabama border post [[25°64'19"S-25°57'42"E].

Opening times are: 06h00 – 22h00
Telephone: +27-18-390 2533

The above routes should not take more than five hours (to the border posts).

From Cape Town join the N7 highway to Springbok. (Watch out for tortoises and other scaly fauna crossing the freeway!) From Springbok take the N14 highway past Upington to Kuruman. You may then head on for Hotazel on the R380 regional road and McCarthy's Rest border post [26°20'15"S-22°56'79"E].

Opening hours are: 06h00 – 18h00
Telephone: +27-53-781 0285

The following route is a convenient alternative route to Zimbabwe, as it helps one avoid the congestion at Beitbridge!! From Pretoria take the N1 highway past Mokgophong to Mokopane. From there take the N11 highway route past Baltimore to Martin's Drift/ Groblersbrug border post [22°99'81"S-27°94'19"E].

Opening times are: 08h00 – 22h00
Telephone: +27-14—767 1019

SA BORDER WITH LESOTHO

The most convenient entry into this mountainous country is through Bloemfontein-which is easily reachable from Johannesburg directly on through the N1 highway. From there the N8 highway takes you to Ladybrand and-ten minutes later-to the Maseru Bridge border post [29°29'80"S-27°45'46"E]. Maseru City is a spitting distance from the border post.

Opening times are: 24hours everyday
Telephone: +27-51-924 4300

To avoid holiday congestion at Maseru bridge border post, one may use Ficksburg Bridge/Maputsoe border post [28°88'39"S-27°89'03"E] as its open 24hours daily.

Route

Leave the N1 highway at Kroonstad and head for Senekal either directly past Steynsrus or drive past Winburg and then for Marquard, Clocolan AND then ease into Ficksburg. Maseru is a shade below 90km from Ficksburg.

For coastal towns and cities like Cape Town, George, Knysna, Port Elizabeth and East London, the easiest access to Lesotho is through the N1 highway-other than from Cape Town-is reached through N12, N9, N10 and N6 higways respectively. From Durban a tortuous route takes you to Port Shepstone on the N2 higway. You will then have to head for Marburg, Harding, Kokstad, Matatiele (on the R56). From here you have to branch off to Ramohlakoana, to enter Lesotho at Qacha' Nek border post [30°12'97"S-28°68'56"E].

Opening times are: 06h00 – 22h00
Telephone: +27-39-256 4391

SA BORDER WITH MOZAMBIQUE

The most convenient port of entry into Mozambique is Lebombo border post [25°44'31"S-31°98'67"E] (called Ressano Garcia on the Mozambican side). From either Johannesburg or Pretoria take the N12 highway past Emalahleni and Nelspruit, a convenient stop over. From here travel past Malelane and find the border post two minutes past Komatipoort, another convenient town for refreshments, et cetera. One minute past the Komatipoort turn off, a filling station and convenience shops are available. Maputo City is a leisurely hour's drive from Ressano Garcia.

Opening times are: 06h00 – 24h00
Telephone: +27-13-793 7311

(This border post often stays open for 24hours during peak holiday periods. Further, transit of trucks has been separated from pedestrian and other motor cars, thus easing passage considerably).

The other three border posts (Giroyondo, Kosi Bay and Pafuri) are more suited to adventure travellers, driving exclusively 4-wheel drive vehicles in the case of Kosi Bay). The Giriyondo [23°58'40"S-31°66'00"E] and Pafuri border posts lead directly into the Great Limpopo Transfrontier Park.

SA BORDER WITH NAMIBIA

From Johannesburg/Pretoria head for Krugersdorp and then take the N14 highway to Vryburg. From there wheeze past Kuruman, Sishen onto Upington. From there take the N10 highway and ease into Nakop border post/Ariamsvlei [28°09'49"S-19°99'92"E] an hour later.

Opening times are: 24hours round the clock.

From Cape Town heading north on the N7 highway will take you to Springbok and then onto Vioolsdrif/Noordoewer border post [28°76'56"S-17°62'62"E].

Opening times are: 24hours round the clock.

For adventure travellers take the Port Nolloth turnoff at Steinkopf and head west for the sea. From there head north to enter Namibia at Alexander Bay/Oranjemund border post [28°56'47"S-16°50'36"E].

Opening times are: 06h00 – 22h00
Telephone and Facsimile: +27-27-831 1662

SA BORDER WITH SWAZILAND

The easiest entry into Swaziland is through the N4 highway to the cold Belfast. From there branch off eastwards along the R33 to Carolina and join the N17 at Warburton, whereafter you'll head past Lochiel and Hartebeeskop [26°08'56"S-30°46'15"E] for the Oshoek/Ngwenya border post [26°21'25"S-30°98'92"E]. The capital city of Mbabane is a leisurely fifteen minutes' drive from the Ngwenya border post.

Opening times are: 07h00 – 22h00
Telephone: +27-17-8820138 or 9

Golela border post is convenient for travellers from Durban. Joining the N2 from Durban is a breeze. It leads one straight into Golela border post [27°31'72"S-31°88'84"E] about four hours later.

Opening times are: 07h00 – 22h00
Telephone: +27-34-435 1070

SA BORDER WITH ZIMBABWE

Other than passing through Botswana, reaching Zimbabwe from Johannesburg/Pretoria (South Africa) is best done by joining the N1highway, past Mokopane and Polokwane, Makhado and then onto Musina. Beit Bridge border post [22°22'43"S-29°98'65"E] is a stone's throw further on.

Opening times are: 24 hours daily
Telephone and facsimile: +27-15-530 0070

GENERAL SERVICES AVAILABLE AT BORDER POSTS

These include:
- Home Affairs, which handles immigration of persons.
- South African Police Services, which offers general assistance in maintaining law and order.
- South African Revenue Services, which controls taxation of imported/exported goods.
- Agricultural inspectorate, which controls importation/ exportation of permitted fauna and flora as well as help in raising awareness of endemic or new animal disease outbreaks.
- Very basic ablutions.

Passports and visas

These are essential documents for passage through border posts. Validity of a passport is of critical importance. At least one page-for safety's sake, two pages-must still be empty (for stamping purposes). South Africans do not need visas when travelling to neighbouring countries which are members of the Southern African Customs Union (SACU).

Third party insurance

Third party insurance is compulsory in all African countries. Commonly, enforcement is lax at some border posts. However, this situation should not be taken advantage of...COMESA insurance ("yellow card") offers compulsory cover for a vehicle in respect of third party liabilities in destination country. This insurance applies

to the following countries: Burundi, Djibouti, Democratic Republic of the Congo, Eritrea, Ethiopia, Kenya, Malawi, Rwanda, Sudan Tanzania, Uganda, Zambia and Zimbabwe. It is available at the Automobile Association of South Africa
(the "AA" +27-11-799 1041 or 2/+27-11- 799 1713. Check the link in our website for other AA branches countrywide).

As an example current costs of third party insurance applicable in Mozambique are:

Category of car	Code	Cost (USD)
Car/sedan	20024	23 (R160.00)
Car + trailer/boat	20167	35 (R240.00)
Motorbike	20025	13 (R90.00)
Heavy commercial vehicles	20029	52 (R360.00)

USAGE OF RENTED CARS ACROSS BORDERS

A letter of authority is mandatory when crossing borders using someone else's car, for instance, rented cars. The same holds true if the car you are driving is still being paid for by way of lease or instalment sale.

Driving cross-border/abroad

It is prudent to acquire an international driving permit when travelling in African countries. It easily available at AA shops in South Africa for about USD42, on production of the vehicle's original registration documents and a certified copy of your identification document. In all countries abutting South Africa cars travel on the left.

Identification stickers include:

- The ZA sticker (black letters on a white background) which must be displayed at the back of your South African car, furthest from the number plate.
- The yellow triangle on a blue background is required when towing a trailer. One sticker must be placed on the front right side of your towing car and the other one on the rear of the trailer being towed.
- In Zimbabwe one white T and on red T, both on a black background are required for towing and towed vehicles respectively, both on the extreme right of both vehicles.
- In Mozambique two red warning triangles are required, as is lime coloured polyester jackets with yellow reflective strips, running from shoulders-on both sides-down to the waist and also around the waist. All these items are available at the AA or in leisure and outdoor shops countrywide.

SOUTH AFRICAN REVENUE SERVICE (SARS) AT BORDER POSTS

SARS' services are available at all border posts detailed above. Relevant contact details are:

National Contact Centre	0800 00 7277
International caller	+27-11-602 2093
Fraud and anti-corruption Hotline	0800 00 2870
Website:	http://www.sars.gov.za

(Guide on Carbon Dioxide (CO_2) emissions is incomplete and has not yet been released).

SARS' currency rates of exchange and are calculable on a daily basis. The single and multiple value charts are available at http://commerce.sats.gov.za/roe/default.htm.

EXCISE DUTIES AND LEVIES PAYABLE

These are payments primarily serve as a revenue collection exercise. Secondarily, they influence consumer behaviour in respect of, for example, personally harmful products like alcohol and cigarettes) as well as environmentally harmful products like plastic bags.

Excise duties are applicable to the following products consumed in countries comprising the Southern African Customs Union (SACU), namely, South Africa, Botswana, Lesotho, Namibia and Swaziland. These are:

1. Specific Excise Duty products like fuel/petroleum products, tobacco products, malt and traditional African beer, wine and other fermented beverages. These goods are assessed based on quantity/volume/mass, irrespective of value thereof;
2. Ad valorem Excise Duty products like motor vehicles, electronic equipment, perfumery items and others. These goods are assessed based on their value.

Each SACU member country are/may impose different levies-fuel levy, Road Accident Fund, Diamond export levy and environment levies-on fuel, road usage, coal and gas import/export as well motor vehicle carbon emissions respectively. Relevant policies, procedures, guides and application forms, are available at every SARS office at the border posts as well as from their website. (http://www.sars.gov.za). To view current rates of Excise duty/levy, relevant links are available too.

Customs procedure on arrival in/departure from South Africa

One has to report to the customs officer at point of entry to declare all the goods purchased abroad in one's possession. Certain items may be transported duty free. These are:

1. Personal effects.
2. New or used goods NOT exceeding USD 400 in value.
3. Less than two litres of wine.
4. Less than one litre of other alcoholic beverages.
5. Less than 200 cigarettes/20 cigars/250 grams cigarette tobacco per person. Exclude children under eighteen years of age).
6. Less than 50millilitres (ml) of perfumery/250ml toilet water.

All the above items are Value Added Tax (VAT) exempt. Goods imported for business/commercial purposes do NOT qualify for the above allowances. Such allowances may only be claimed once per person during a period of 30days and if returning after an absence of 48hours. Firearms are expressly excluded from this provision-especially when being imported by returning residents after an absence of less than six months. Firearm transit is handled by Customs personnel in conjunction with relevant South African Police Services (SAPS) personnel.

Anti-dumping and countervailing duties are levied on goods considered to be "dumped" in South Africa or subsidised imported goods.

Value Added Tax (VAT)

Section 7(1) (b) of the Value-Added Tax Act number 89 of 1991 levies VAT at a rate of 14% on the importation of goods into

South Africa from export countries including SACU members. Section 13(3) of the Act-read with schedule 1-exempts certain imported goods from VAT. The amount and type of duty imposed on a product is determined by the customs value of the goods, the volume/quantity of the goods and their tariff classification.

Customs values are set by the General Agreement on Tariffs and Trade (GATT) valuation code, which involves six valuation methods. The majority of goods are valued using method one, which is the actual price paid or payable by the buyer of the goods. The "free on board" (FOB) price forms the basis for the value, but allows for certain deductions (such as interest charged on extended payment terms) and additions, for instance, royalties. The duty payable may be increased based on the assessment by the customs official on the relationship between the buyer and the seller, payments outside normal business transactions (such as royalties and licence fees) and restrictions placed on the buyer.

Certain rebates, such as industrial rebates, are available on goods that meet specific criteria and have been imported for a specific industry. General rebates may apply if goods have been imported:

- temporarily;
- for repair;
- as passenger's baggage;
- for local manufacturing destined for the export market only.

Flat-rate assessment

In addition to duty-free allowance, a traveller/passenger may elect to pay customs duty at a flat rate of 20% on goods that have been acquired abroad/in any duty-free shop. These additional goods-new or used, qualify for this concession if their value does not exceed

R12 000.00 (USD 1600). For cargo arriving at a South African border post, a cargo manifest must reflect all the imported goods.

Motor vehicle importation

Natural persons may, on changing their residence to South Africa on a permanent basis (sanctioned by the Department of Home Affairs), import one motor vehicle free of duty and exempt from VAT. South African working/studying abroad do NOT qualify for this rebate. Motor vehicles used by tourists in South Africa may be imported under rebate of duty and exempt from VAT for a period of three months. An extension of up to six months is allowable, subject to a provisional payment made to Customs to secure the VAT on importation either in part or in full. After six months the motor vehicle must be re-exported.

Prohibited goods

It's illegal to bring the following goods to South Africa:

1. Narcotics, psychotropic substances as well as habit-forming drugs such as cannabis, heroin, cocaine, Mandrax, Ecstasy and any paraphernalia referring to it.
2. Firearms, weapons and ammunition.
3. Poison and other toxic substances.
4. Cigarettes with a mass of more than 2kg per 1000.
5. Goods to which a trade description or trademark is applied in contravention of any Act, for instance, counterfeit goods.
6. Unlawful reproductions of any works subject to copyright.
7. Prison-made and penitentiary-made goods.

Goods that have to be declared

1. South African bank notes in excess of R5000.00, gold coins, coin and stamp collections and unprocessed gold.

2. Endangered plants and animals-alive or dead.

3. Food, plants, animals and biological goods.

4. Medicines: Travellers are allowed to bring one month's supply of pharmaceutical drugs and medicines for their personal use. All other medicines or pharmaceutical drugs have to be declared and have to be accompanied by a letter or certified prescription from a registered physician.

Chapter Two

COMMUNICATION SERVICES

For travellers it is essential to know how to mobilise communication services whilst in transit through South African borders. Adventure travellers can now make use of a combination satellite/GPS phone with Immersat technology. However, an ordinary mobile suffices for making and receiving telephone calls. For those mobile phones with further technological enhancements (internet and GPS capabilities) data transfer can easily be performed, as is internet banking or purchasing goods online.

TELEPHONE CODES

Telephone codes are often quoted with a plus prefix, that is, the sign +. This sign is then followed by a country code, which should precede the number you may want to call. These codes are most useful when phoning numbers whilst you are outside your destination country. Even once you are within your destination country, complete codes are still operational, though not necessary. Two zeroes may also be used instead of the plus sign. The specific codes are:

Country	Country code
Botswana	+267 3 (002673)
Lesotho	+266 2 (00266 2)
Mozambique	+258 (00258)
Namibia	+264 (00264)
South Africa	+27 (0027)
Swaziland	+268 7 (00268 7)
Zimbabwe	+263 4 (00263 4)

Example:

Once you are within the borders of your destination country, phone any local number using the area code (different from the country code) in full, followed by the number. The landline number for the Cape Town office of South African Airways is 021-936 3366 (area code and then the number), which you may ring as is, if you are anywhere inside South Africa. To phone them whilst you are outside South Africa you'd then ring +27-21-936 3366, and you'll go through. Ringing 0027-21-936 3366 puts you through as well. The same holds true for mobile phone numbers.

HOLIDAYS UNIQUE TO SOUTH AFRICA AND HER NEIGHBOURS

Generally, holidays falling on a Saturday are celebrated on that day. Holidays that fall on a Sunday are celebrated on the following Monday.

South African Holidays

Human Rights Day	(21st March)
Freedom Day	(27th April)
Workers Day	(01st May)
Youth Day	(16th June)
National Women's Day	(09th August)

| Heritage Day | (24th September) |
| Day of Reconciliation | (16th December) |

Botswana Holidays

Ascension Day	(13th May)
Sir Seretse Khama Day	(01st July)
President's Day	(19th July)
Botswana Day	(30th September)

Lesotho Holidays (also called Bank Holidays)

Moshoeshoe Day	(11th March)
Earth Day	(22nd April)
Labour Day	(01st May)
Africa/Heroes Day	(25th May)
Ascension Day	(02nd June)
Kings Anniversary	(17th July)
Independence Day	(04th October)
United Nations Day	(24th October)
Universal Children's Day	(24th November)
Human Rights Day	(10th December)

Mozambican Holidays

Mozambique's Heroes Day	(03rd February)
Mozambique's Women's Day	(07th April)
Labour Day	(01st May)
Independence Day	(25th June)
Lusaka Agreement Day/Victory Day	(7th September)
Armed Forces Day	(25th September)
(A major road next to the harbour is also called Avenida 25 de Setembro)	
Peace/National Reconciliation Day	(04th October)
Family Day	(25th December)

Namibian Holidays

Independence Day	(21st March)
Workers' Day	(01st May)
Cassinga Day	(04th May)
Africa Day	(25th May)
Heroes Day	(26th August)
Human Rights Day	(10th December)

Swaziland Holidays

[The exact dates for Incwala Day (December/January) and Umhlanga/Reed Dance (August/September) are formally announced annually].

King's Birthday	(19th April)
Labour Day	(01st May)
Ascension Day	(02nd June)
Public Holiday	(22nd July)
Somhlolo Day	(06th September)

Zimbabwean Holidays

Independence Day	(18th April)
Workers' Day	(01st May)
Africa Day	(25th May)
Public Women's Day and Children's	
Day Forever Forget Never Out	(02nd July)
Heroes' Day	(2nd Monday in August)
Armed Forces Day	(2nd Tuesday in August)
Unity Day	(22nd December)

Chapter Three

CONSULAR SERVICES

Consular services are services offered by a sovereign country to its nationals who work, live or travel abroad. Ordinarily, such services are available 24hours a day, seven days a week. South Africa's consular services unit supports at least 113 Representatives in at least 100 countries. Not all countries of the world have representatives in SACU member countries. It is therefore of critical importance for the travellers crossing South African borders to acquaint themselves with consular services that are available in countries neighbouring South Africa.

Further, even when a country has formal representation in SACU member countries, not all critical consular services may be available in each and every one of those countries. For comparison's sake here are the consular services available to South Africans abroad:

Emergency services

- Assistance in evacuation planning abroad in cases of political turmoil, natural and man-made disasters. The nature of the disaster and safety considerations could influence the ability to respond. "Evacuation from a location abroad is not a right that can be claimed from the South African government".

- In the event of an emergency communication with the traveller's next of kin will be implanted.
- Provision of non-financial assistance for repatriation and urgently needed medical or professional attention.
- Liason with local authorities to search for and locate missing persons abroad.
- Facilitation of funds transfer to relieve distress abroad.
- Provision of support services and advice in cases of hostage taking, kidnapping or abduction.
- Assistance for South Africans detained/arrested/jailed abroad is offered under the Vienna Convention on Consular Relations (1963), which allows for persons arrested outside their own country access to their consular representative. This standard holds true for member countries only. Signatories commit themselves to treating incarcerated people humanely. Conversely, torture, inhumane or degrading treatment or punishment has to be reported and taken up with the local authorities. Consular services available to South Africans arrested/detained abroad include:
- Establishment and maintenance of contact with and verification of South African citizenship soonest.
- Provision of general information about the legal system of the country of arrest as well as observance of the laws and regulations of the arresting state.
- Undertake prison visits whose frequency depends on current policy, location of the prison, culture and laws of the arresting State, the prevailing security situation in the country and/or the prison and subject to the Mission's operational circumstances.

- Facilitate contact with family/friends with certain limitations and conditions.
- Assist with funds transfer at a maximum of R 2000.00 per month per detainee/prisoner from friends/designated family members.
- Ensure that medical conditions are brought to the attention of the prison authorities. Medicines may be brought by relatives to the consular office for dispatch to the detainee, provided this action does not violate/contradict the rules of the detention facility of the arresting country. Permitted medicines are chargable by weight.
- Dispatch of mail/letters from relatives and friends in open/unsealed and addressed envelopes.
- Facilitate payment for a flight ticket when the detainee is released and is free to go home.

Procedure to access consular services

Contact the nearest embassy representative of your own country or the Chief Director: Consular services in your own country office.

Services NOT available from the South African Consular department

- Institution of court proceedings;
- Dispensing legal advice;
- Organizing release from prison or to make bail applications;
- Travel to dangerous areas or prisons for prison visits;
- Crime investigation;
- Obtain better treatment in prison better than that provided for local nationals. In cases where the United Nations Standard Minimum Rules for the Treatment of Prisoners are not applied/met, the mission will make representation to the relevant local authorities on behalf of the detainee/prisoner;

- Instruct next-of-kin or friends to transfer money;
- Pay legal, medical or any other bills;
- Obtain accommodation, work, visas or residence permits;
- Undertake work done by travel agents, airlines, banks or car rental companies;
- Formally assist dual nationals in the country of their second nationality;
- Pay for the preparation, transport, burial or cremation of the mortal remains of a South African who has died in foreign soil.

Legal and Notary services include:

- Facilitation of the serving of legal summons on defendants abroad;
- Conveyance of requests for extradition, rogatory letters and evidence on commission between states;
- Authentication of public documents for use between states;

Other services

Trade agreements (for business travellers). South Africa has signed many trade agreements with its trading partners (several African countries) in the past few years. Hence, South Africa is a beneficiary of a number of trade arrangements with the European Union and Zimbabwe. These are:

- The African Growth and Opportunity Act (AGOA)
- Trade Agreement between the European Union (EU) and South Africa
- The Southern African Development Community (SADC) Trade Agreement
- The Generalised System of Preferences.

- Trade Agreement between Zimbabwe and South Africa
- Trade Agreement between Southern African Customs Union (SACU) and the European Free Trade Association (EFTA) states
- Rules of Origin Guides/Trade Agreements
- Approved Exporter (SAEU, SACU, EFTA)

FOREIGN EMBASSIES AND CONSULATES IN COUNTRIES NEIGHBOURING SOUTH AFRICA

FOREIGN EMBASSIES/CONSULATES IN BOTSWANA

Embassy of Angola:
153 Nelson Mandela Road, Kapamyo, Gaborone
Telephone: (+267) 390 0204

Embassy of Austria:
Plot 50667, Block B3, Fairground Holdings Park, Gaborone.
Telephone: (+267) 395 15 14

Honorary Consulate of Belgium:
Plot 8503, Quartz Road, Broadhurst, Gaborone.
Telephone: (+267) 395 77 85 and (+267) 395 77 89

Embassy of Brazil:
3rd floor Main Mall, Standard House. Lot 1124, Gaborone.
Telephone: (+267) 395 1061 and (+267) 395 1062

Consulate of Canada:
Vision Hire Building, Queens Road, Gaborone.
Tel.(+2711) 3904411

Embassy of China:
Plot 3096, North Ring Road, Gaborone.

Embassy of Cuba:
Plot 5198, Shakawe Close, Plot 5198, The Village, Gaborone.
Telephone: (+267) 391 1485

Danish Consulate:
Plot 10242, Lejara Road, Broadhurst, Gaborone.
Telephone: 3535 05

Finnish Consulate:
Plot 54123, New Lobatse Road, Gaborone.
Telephone: (+267) 3916195

Embassy of France:
761 Robinson Road, Gaborone.
Telephone: (+267) 397 3863

Embassy of Germany:
Professional House, Segodisane Way, Gaborone.
Telephone: (+267) 395 3143

Guyana Honorary Consulate:
Plot 5679, Broadhurst Industrial Estates, Gaborone.
Telephone: (+267) 391 2655

Indian Consulate:
Plot 5375, President's Drive, Gaborone.
Telephone: (+267) 397 2676

Irish Honorary Consulate:
Honorary Consul (Mr Barney O'Reilly) handles Irish diplomatic representation in Botswana but is based in Maputo. Breffini House, Plot 88, Gaborone International Business Park.
Tel (+267) 3905 807 and 395 3077

Italian Honorary Consulate:
Plot 3090, North Ring Road, Gaborone.
Telephone: (+267) 391 2641

Jamaican Consulate:
PO Box 47053 Gaborone.
Tel (+267) 365 0156 or (+267) 71307750

Kenyan High Commission:
Plot 786, Independence Avenue, Gaborone.
Tel (+267) 395 1408 or 30

Namibian High Commision:
Main Hall, 02nd floor, Debswana House, Gaborone.
Tel (+267) 390 2181

Dutch Consulate:
2698 Phiri Crescent, Gaborone.
Tel (+267) 390 2194

Embassy of Russia:
Tawana Close 4711, Gaborone.
Tel (+267) 395 3389

Embassy of Sweden:
NDB Building, 04th floor, The Mall, Gaborone.
Tel (+267) 395 3912

Embassy of Taiwan:
(Refer To 1.6 that is, Chinese Embassy)

Thailand Consulate:
22358 Semowane Road, Gaborone West Phase IV.
Tel (+267) 390 6818

British High Commission:
Plot 1079- 1084, Main Mall, off Queens Road, Gaborone.
Tel (+267) 395 2841

Embassy of the USA:
see http://gaborone.embassy.gov/
Tel (+267) 395 3982

Zambian High Commission:
Plot 1118, The Mall, Gaborone.
Tel (+267) 395 1951/2/3

Zimbabwean High Commission:
Plot 8850, Gaborone.
Tel (+267) 3914495

FOREIGN EMBASSIES/CONSULATES IN LESOTHO

Canadian Consulate:
3 Orpen Road, Old Europa, Maseru.
Tel (+266) 22 315365

Embassy of China:
United Nations Road, Maseru.
Tel (00266) 22 316521

Danish Consulate:
Site 16, Mohlomi Road, Maseru.
Tel (00266) 22 313630

German Honorary Consul:
70C Maluti Road, Maseru West.
Tel (00266) 22 332983

Embassy of Ireland:
Tona-Kholo Road, Maseru West 100.
Tel (00266) 22 314 068

Dutch Consulate:
Lancers Inn, Maseru.
Tel (00266) 22 312114

Pakistani Honorary Consulate:
314 Matlaka Road, New Europa, Maseru.
Tel (00266) 22 312 501 and 22 311 751

Embassy of the USA:
254 Kingsway, Maseru.
Tel. (00266) 22 312 666

FOREIGN EMBASSIES/CONSULATES IN MOZAMBIQUE

Embassy of Algeria:
121 – 125 BP 1709 Rue de Mukumbura, Maputo.
Tel (00258) 1 49 2070 or (00258) 1 49 22 03

Embassy of Angola:
783 Avenida Kenneth Kaunda, CP 2954, Maputo.
Tel (00258) 21 493 139

Australian Honorary Consulate:
95 Third floor, Avenida Zedequias Manganhela, Maputo.
Tel. (00258) 1 322 780

Austrian Consulate:
2761 Av 24 de Julho, 4, Maputo.
Tel (+258) 21 323 32 14 or (+258) 21 42 99 78

Belgian Honorary Consulate:
470 Av Kenneth Kaunda, Maputo.
Tel (+258) 21 492 009

Embassy of Brazil: 296 Av Kenneth Kaunda, Maputo.
Tel (+258) 21 48 48 00 and 01 (direto di embaixadora)

Canadian High Commision:
1138, Av Kenneth Kaunda, Maputo.
Tel (+258) 21492 623

Embassy of China:
3142, Av Julius Nyerere, Maputo.
Tel (+258)21 491560200

Embassy of Cuba:
492 Av Kenneth Kaunda, Maputo.
Tel (+258) 21 49 244

Cypriot Honorary Consulate:
465 Av Paolo Samuel Kankhumba, Maputo.
Tel (00258) 21 497 373 or mobile phone (00258) 21 82 3063850

Czech Republic Honorary Consulate:
190 Rua Estevao Dom Ataide, Maputo.
Tel (00258) 21 497395

Embassy of Denmark:
1162 Av Julius Nyerere, Maputo.
Tel (00258) 21 480000
Faroe Islands and Greenland are part of the Denmark Kingdom.

Embassy of Egypt:
851 Av Mao Tse Tung, Maputo.

Tel (00258) 21 491 118 or 491 287

Embassy of Finland:
1128 Av Julius Nyerere.
Tel. (00258) 21 490 578 or 482 400

Embassy of France:
2361 Av Julius Nyerere.
Tel (00258) 21 484 600

Embassy of Germany.
506 Rua Damiao de Gois, Maputo.
Tel. (00258)21 482 700 or 492 714

Honorary Consulate of Greece:
Third floor, Block IV, Time Square Office Park, Av de Setembro, Maputo.
Tel (00258) 21 310 610 to 2.

Embassy of Iceland:
1694 Av Zimbabwe, Maputo.
Tel (00258) 1 483 509

High Commission of India.
167 Av Kenneth Kaunda.
Tel (00258) 1 492 437 or 490 717
5.1 Honorary Consulate of Indonesia: 1109 Av Agostino Neto, Maputo.
Tel   (00258) 21 310 831

Embassy of Ireland:
3332 Av Julius Nyerere, Maputo.
Tel (00258) 21 491 440

Embassy of Italy:
387 Av Kenneth Kaunda.

Tel. (00258) 1 492229
Honorary Consulate of Madagascar:
20 Av dos Presidentes, Maputo.
Tel (0025821) 486 490

Embassy of Malawi:
75 Av Kenneth Kaunda, Maputo.
Tel (0025821) 491 468 or 492 676

High Commission for Mauritius:
Rue Dom Carlos, No 42 Av de Zimbabwe, Sommerschield, Maputo.
Tel (00258210 494 624 or 494 182.

Embassy of The Netherlands:
324 Av Kwame Nkrumah, Maputo.
Tel (0025821) 484 200

c/o Caminhos de Ferro de Mozambique, Beira.
Tel (0025823) 322 735

36A Rua de Inhambane, Bairro Muhavire, Nampula Province,
Mozambique.
Tel (0025826) 212 970 or 218 615

Embassy of Norway:
CP 828, 1162 Av Julius Nyerere, Maputo.
Tel (0025821) 480100/2/3/4

Embassy of The Palestine:
Maputo
Tel (00258)4 860571

Honorary Consulate of Poland:
39 Rua Clarim de Chaves, Maputo.
Tel 90025821) 329 111

Embassy of Russia:
CP 4666, 2445 Av Vladimir Lenine, Maputo.
Tel (0025821) 417 372 or 419 872 or 418 478

Consulate of Seychelles:
213 Rua de Mesquita, Maputo.
Tel (0025821) 313 744 or 322 060 or 313 032 or 493 813 or
(00258) 823261190 (Mobile)

Consulate of Slovakia.
Rua Comandante Joao Belo, 228 Independence Drive, Maputo.
Tel (00258) 1 311 009

Embassy of Spain: 347 Rua Damiao de Gois, Maputo.
Tel (00258) 1 492 025 or 492 027 or 492 030.

Swaziland High Commission:
Av Kwame Nkrumah, Maputo.
Tel (00258) 1 491 721 or 491 601

Embassy of Sweden:
1128 Av Julius Nyerere, Maputo.
Tel (0025821) 480 300

Embassy of Tanzania:
Ujama House, Maputo.
Tel (00263) 4 721 870 or 722 627 or 882 265

Embassy of the USA:
193 Av Kenneth Kaunda, Maputo.
Tel (0025821) 492 797
Embassy of Zambia:
1286 Av Kenneth Kaunda.
Tel (0025821) 491 307 or 492 452

Embassy of Zimbabwe:

Zimbabwe Consulate General: 617 Rua Francisco Dechage Almelda, Beira, Maputo.

Tel (0025821) 490 699 or 490 404 or 490025

FOREIGN EMBASSIES/CONSULATES IN NAMIBIA

Embassy of Angola:

Ausspan Street 3, Angola House, Windhoek.

Tel ((+264 61) 227 535

Consulate of Angola in Rundu, Namibia

Tel (00264 66) 255782

Embassy of Angola in Oshakati, Namibia.

Tel (00264 65) 221799

Austrian Consulate:

Teinert Strase 2, Windhoek:

Tel (00264 61) 375 652

High Commission of Botswana:

Windhoek

Tel (00264 61) 221941/7

Honorary Consulate of Bulgaria:

Tel (00264 61) 246 333

Consulate of Canada:

4 Eadir Street,Windhoek.

Tel (00264 61) 251 254.

Services are offered through their Hich Commission in Pretoria, South Africa.

Embassy of China:

13 Wecke Street, Windhoek.

Tel (00264 61) 372 800

Embassy of Cuba:
31 Omuramba Road, Windhoek.
Tel (00264 61) 22 7072

Honorary Consulate of Cyprus:
Venus Building, 60 Sam Nujoma Avenue, Windhoek.
Tel (00264 64) 204 501 or 207030 (direct) or mobile:
(+264 81 1294501)

Consulate of Denmark:
7 Best Street, (IBIS Namibia) Windhoek.
Tel (00264 61) 237 565

Embassy of Egypt:
10 Berg Street, Klein Windhoek, Windhoek.
Tel (0026461) 221501

Embassy of Finland:
2 Crohn Street, corner Bahnhof Street), Windhoek.
Tel (00264 61) 221 355

Consulate of Finland:
Mindset Investments, 32 Rikumbi Kandanga Road, Walvis Bay.
Tel (00264 64) 207 232

Embassy of France:
1 Goethe Street, Windhoek.
Tel (00264 61) 276700

Embassy of Germany:
6F Sanlam Centre, Independence Avenue, Windhoek.
Tel. (00264 61) 273100 or 273133

Honorary Hungarian Consulate:
7 Hippokrates Street, Windhoek West, Windhoek.
Tel (00264 61) 223 175/ Mobile: (00264 81 124 7493

High Commissioner for India:
97 Nelson Mandela Avenue, Windhoek.
Tel. (00264 61) 226 037

Embassy of Indonesia:
103 Nelson Mandela Avenue, Windhoek.
Tel (00264 61) 285 1000

Embassy of Italy:
Corner Anna and Gevers Streets, Ludwigdorf, Windhoek.
Tel (00264 61) 228 602

High Commission of Kenya.
134 Robert Mugabe Avenue, Windhoek.
Tel. (00264 61) 225 900 or 226836

Embassy of Malawi.
56 Bismarck Street, Windhoek.
Tel (00264 61) 221 391/2/3

High Commission of Malaysia.
12 Baba Street, Ludwigsdorf, Windhoek.
Tel (00264 61) 259 342 or 259 344

Consulate of Netherlands.
Unit 4, 18 Liliencron Street, Windhoek.
Tel (00264 61) 223733

Consulate of New Zealand.
23 Bodin Street, Pioneers Park, Academiam, Windhoek.
Tel (00264 61) 225 228

Embassy of Russia.
4 Christian Street, Windhoek.
Tel (00264 61) 228 671

Embassy of Spain:
58 Bismarck Street, Windhoek.
Tel (00264 61) 223 066 or 224 038 or 224 000

Embassy of Sudan:
6 Johanna Albrecht Street, Windhoek.
Tel (00264 61) 228 544

Embassy of Sweden:
9th Floor, Sanlam Centre, 154 Independence Avenue, Windhoek.
Tel (00264 61) 258 278 / Fax (+264) 230 528

Embassy of Venezuela:
10th Floor, Sanlam Centre, 154 Independence Avenue, Windhoek.
Tel (00264 61) 227 905 or 227 907

Embassy of Zambia:
22 Sam Nujoma Drive, Corner of Mandume Ndemufayo Avenue, Windhoek.
Tel (00264 61) 237 610 or 237 611

Embassy of Zimbabwe:
(Physical address undetermined)
Tel (00264 61) 228 134 or 228 137 or 227738

FOREIGN EMBASSIES/CONSULATES IN SWAZILAND

Embassy of Canada.
(The Government of Canada has no resident representation in Swaziland. Services are offered through its High Commission in Pretoria)

Honorary Consulate of the Republic of Cyprus:

Villa Zuan Building, Corner of Kholwane Road and Lituba Avenue, Mbabane, Swaziland.

Tel (00268) 2404 2650/ Mobile: (+268) 76037096 (Mobile)

Consulate of Denmark:

CDC Sokhamlilo Building, Corner of Johnson and Walker Street, Mbabane, Swaziland.

Tel (+268) 2 404 3547

Honorary Consulate of Finland:

Guava Gallery, Twiga Estate, Mantenga, Ezulwini Valley, Mbabane.

Tel (00268)2 416 2912 or 2 4161 343

Honorary Consulate of Indonesia:

Union Suppliers, H 100 Mbabane.

High Commission of Mozambique:

Highlands View, Princess Drive Road, Mbabane.

Tel (00268) 2 404 3700 or 404 1296 or 7

Consulate of Netherlands:

Swaziland Contract Furnishers Building, Siguca Street, Mbabane Industrial Estate, Mbabane.

Tel (00268) 2 404 5178

Embassy of Taiwan:

Makhosikhosi Street, Mbabane.

Tel (00268) 2 404 4739/40/41

Honorary British Consulate:

Frank Pettit, Eveni H103, Mbabane.

United States of America Embassy:
7th Floor, Central Bank Building, Mahlokohla Street, Mbabane.
Tel (00268) 2 404 6441

FOREIGN EMBASSIES/CONSULATES IN ZIMBABWE

Embassy of Algeria:
8 Pascoe Avenue, Harare.
Tel (002634) 791 773 or 791 791

Embassy of Angola:
26 Speke Avenue, Doncaster House, Harare.
Tel (002634) 770 075 or 770 076

Embassy of Australia:
1 Green Close, Borrowdale, Harare.
Tel (002634) 852 471 or 852 511

Embassy of Austria:
13 Duthie Road, Alexander Park, Harare.
Tel (002634) 702 921 or 702 922

Embassy of Belgium:
5th Floor Tanganyika House, 23 Third Street/ corner of Union
Avenue, Harare.
Tel (002634) 790 307 or 793 306

Embassy of Botswana:
22 Phillips Avenue, Belgravia, Harare.
Tel 9002634) 729 551 or 793 492 or 3

Embassy of Brazil:
9th Floor Old Mutual Centre, Corner Third Street and Jason Moyo
Avenue, Harare.
Tel (002634) 790 740 or 790 741

Embassy of Bulgaria:
15 Maasdorp Avenue, Alexander Park, Harare.
Tel (002634) 730 509

Embassy of Canada:
45 Baines Avenue, Harare.
Tel (002634) 252 181 or 252 183 or 252 185

Embassy of China:
58 Golden Stairs Road, Mount Pleasant, Harare.
Tel (002634) 332 760/1/2

Embassy of Cyprus:
15 Braemar Avenue, Northwood.
Tel (002634) 301 903 or +263 11 200119 (Mobile)

Embassy of the Czech Republic:
4 Sandringham Drive, Harare,
Tel (002634) 700 636

Embassy of Egypt:
7 Aberdeen Road, Avondale, Harare.
Tel (002634) 303 445 or 303 497

Embassy of Ethiopia:
14 Lanark Road, Belgravia, Harare.
Tel (002634) 725 822 or 725 823

Embassy of Finland:
4 Duthie Road, Alexander Park, Harare.
Tel (002634) 751 654 or 752 931

Embassy of France:
11th Floor Bank Chambers, 76 Samora Machel Avenue, Harare.
Tel (002634) 703 216 or 704 069

Embassy of Germany:
30 Ceres Road, Avondale, Harare.
Tel (002634) 308 655

Embassy of Greece:
8 Deary Avenue, Belgravia, Harare.
Tel (002634) 793 208 or 723 747

High Commission of India:
12 Natal Road, Belgravia, Harare.
Tel (002634) 795 955 or 795 956

Embassy of Indonesia:
3 Duthie Road, Belgravia, Harare.
Tel (002634) 251 799 or 250 072

Honorary Consulate of Ireland:
Lamont House, 2 Robert Mugabe Road, Harare.
Tel (002634) 771 949

Embassy of Italy:
7 Bartholomew Close, Greendale, Harare.
Tel (002634) 497 200

Embassy of Japan:
4th Floor Social Security Center, Corner Julius Nyerere Way and
Sam Nujoma Street, Harare.
Tel (002634) 250 025 or 7

High Commission of Kenya:
95 Park Lane, Harare.
Tel (002634) 704 820 or 704 833 or 704 637.

Embassy of Kuwait:
1 Bath Road, Belgravia, Harare.

Tel (002634) 733 351/2/3

High Commission of Malawi:
9 – 11 Duthie Road, Alexandra Park, Harare.
Tel (002634) 798 584 or 7

Embassy of Malaysia:
40 Downie Avenue, Avondale, Harare.
Tel (002634) 334 413 or 334 414

High Commission of Mozambique:
152 Herbert Chitepo Avenue, Harare.
Tel (002634) 253 871 or 3

High Commission of Namibia:
Lot 1 of 7A, Borrowdale Estates, 69 Borrowdale Road, Harare.
Tel (002634) 885 841

Embassy of Norway:
5 Lanark Road, Belgravia, Harare.
Tel (002634) 252 426

Embassy of Pakistan:
11 Van Praagh Avenue, Milton Park, Harare.
Tel (002634) 720 293 or 794 264

Embassy of Palestine:
1 Fairbridge Avenue, Belgravia, Harare.
Tel (002634) 794 330

Embassy of Romania:
105 Fourth Street, corner of Josiah Street, Chinamano, Harare.
Tel (002634) 790 559 or 700 853

Embassy of Russia:
70 Fife Avenue, Harare.
Tel (002634) 701 957 or 701 958

Embassy of Serbia:
1 Lanark Road, Harare.
Tel (002634) 251 592 or 251 593

Embassy of Slovakia:
35 Aberdeen Road, Harare.
Tel (002634) 302 636 or 307 238 or 307 239

Embassy of Korea:
3rd Floor Eastgate Building, Redbridge, Corner Third Street and
Robert Mugabe Road, Harare.
Tel (002634) 756 541 or 4

Embassy of Spain:
16 Phillips Avenue, Belgravia, Harare.
Tel (002634) 738 681 or 738 682 or 3.

Embassy of Sudan:
4 Pascoe Avenue, Avondale, Harare.
Tel (002634) 700 111

Embassy of Sweden:
32 Aberdeen Road, Avondale, Harare:
Tel (002634) 302 636

Embassy of Tanzania:
Ujama House, 23 Baines Avenue, Harare.
Tel (002634) 721 870 or 722 627 or 882 265

Embassy of Great Britain:
7th Floor Corner House, Corner Samora Machel Avenue and

Leopold Takawira Street, Harare.
Tel (002634) 772 990 or 774 700

Embassy of the USA:
172 Herbert Chitepo Avenue Harare.
Tel (002634) 250 593 or 4

High Commission of Zambia:
Zambia House, Union Avenue, Harare.
Tel (002634) 790 851

Chapter Four

FOREIGN REPRESENTATION IN SOUTH AFRICA

This section seeks to inform residents/nationals of countries that do not have diplomatic representation in countries neighbouring South Africa. Names of consular personnel are available but not included herein as these may change at short notice. Some of the senior designations are vacant.

Albania (Republic of):
Shop G57, Fourways Mall, Sandton 2055 (Johannesburg).
Tel (+27) 11-465 3871 (National Day: 28 November)

Algeria (Democratic People's Republic of):
950 Arcadia Street, Hatfield, 0083 (Pretoria).
Tel (+2712) 342 5074 or 75 or 342 6345/Telex: 320078
EMBAL SA (National Day: 5 July

Angola (Republic of):
1030 Schoeman Street, Hatfield, 0083 (Pretoria).

Tel (+2712) 342 0049 or 50 or 342 4404 or 342 3696 or 342 3671 or 342 9377.

Consulate General in Johannesburg:
Goud and 334 Bree Street, Johannesburg, 2001.
Tel (+2711) 333 2721or 5.

Consulate General (Durban):
324 Florida Road, Morningside, Durban, 4001.
Tel (+2731) 312 6516 (National Day: 11 November)

Argentine Republic:
200 Standard Plaza, 440 Hilda Street, Hatfield, 0083 (Pretoria).
Tel(+2712) 430 3524 or 7 or 430 2907 (National Day: 25 May)

Australia:
292 Orient Street, Corner Schoeman Street, Arcadia, 0083. (Pretoria).
Tel (+2712) 423 6000 (24 hours).

Commercial Office in Johannesburg:
10th Floor The Forum, Corner Maud and 5th Streets, Sandton, 2146.
Tel (+2711) 911 4500. (National Day: 26 January)

Austria (Republic of):
1109 Duncan Street, Brooklyn, 0181.
Tel (+2712) 452 9155.

Commercial Office in Johannesburg:
2nd Floor Cradock Heights, 21 Cradock Avenue, Rosebank, 2196. Tel (+2711) 442 7100 (National Day: 26 October)

Bangladesh (People's Republic of):
410 Farenden Street, Sunnyside, 0002.
Tel (+2712) 343 2105 to 7. (National Day: 26 March)

Belarus (Republic of):
327 Hill Street, Arcadia, 0002.
Tel (+2712) 430 7664 or 7707 to 9 (National Day: 3 July)

Belgium (Kingdom of):
625 Leyds Street, Muckleneuk, 0002.
Tel (+2712) 440 3201 or 2.

> Consulate General in Johannesburg:
> 3rd Floor West Core, 158 Jan Smuts Avenue/9 Walters, Rosebank, 2196.

> Consulate General in Cape Town:
> 4th Floor Vogue House, Thibault Square, Foreshore, 8001.
> Tel (+2721) 419 4690. (National Day: 21 July)

Benin (Republic of):
900 Park Street, Corner Park and Orient Streets, Arcadia, 0007.
Tel (+2712) 342 6978. (National Day: 1 August)

Bolivia (Republic of):
2 Meadowbrook Close, French Lane, Morningside, 2196.
Tel (+2711) 883 3416.

> Consulate in Cape Town:
> 2nd Floor Safmarine House, 22 Riebeeck Street, Cape Town.
> Tel(+2721) 421 4040/1/2 (National Day: 7 September)

Bulgaria (Republic of):
1071 Church Street, Hatfiled, 0083.
Tel (+2712) 342 3720 or21. (National Day: 3 March)

Burkina Faso:
49 Charles Street, Bailey's Muckleneuk, (Pretoria).
Tel (+2712) 346 6205 or 346 2704. (National Day: 11 December)

Burundi (Republic of):

20 Glyn Street, Pretoria.
Tel (+2712) 342 4881 or 4883 (National Day: 4 July)

Botswana (Republic of):

24 Amos Street, Colbyn, 0083.
Tel (+2712) 430 9640.

> Consulate General in Johannesburg:
> 2nd Floor Future Bank Building, 122 De Korte Street, Braamfontein, 2001.
> Tel (+2711) 403 3748.

> Consulate General in Cape Town:
> 4th Floor Southern Life Centre, 8 Riebeeck Street, Cape Town, 8000.
> Tel (+2721) 421 1045. (National Day: 30 September)

Brazil (Federative Republic of):

1st Floor Hillcrest Office Park, Woodpecker Place, 177 Dyer Road, Hillcrest, 0083. (Pretoria).
Tel (+2712) 366 5200 (National Day: 7 September)

Cameroon (Republic of):

80 Marais Street, Brooklyn, 0181.
Tel (+2712) 460 0587 (National Day: 20 May)

Canada:

1103 Arcadia Street, Corner Hilda Street, Hatfield, 0083.
Tel (+2712) 422 3000.

> Commercial Office in Johannesburg:
> 1st Floor, Cradock Place, 10 Arnold Road, off Cradock Avenue, Rosebank, 2196.
> Tel (+2711) 442 3130.

> Honorary Consulate in Durban:

25/27 Marriott Road, Durban, 4001.
Tel(+2731) 309 8434 (National Day: 1 July)

Central African Republic:
822 Arcadia Street, Arcadia, Pretoria.
Tel (+2712) 725864700 (National Day: 1 December)

Chad:
412 Charles Street, Brooklyn, 0181.
Tel (+2712) 460 1596.
(National Day: 11 August)

Chile (Republic of):
Delmondo Office Park, 169 Garsfontein Road, Ashley Gardens, 0081. (Pretoria)
Tel (+2712) 460 8090.

Commercial Office in Johannesburg:
1st Floor Building 3, 93 Grayston Drive, Sandton, 2196.
Tel (+2711) 784 8422 or 23.

Consulate General in Cape Town:
19th Floor Suite 1918 Main Tower, Standard Bank Centre, Heerengracht, 8001.
Tel (+2721) 421 2344/46.

Consulate (Honorary) in Durban:
67 Venice Road, Morningside, 4001.
Tel (+2731) 312 8608.
(National Day: 18 September)

China (People's Republic of):
965 Church Street, Arcadia, 0083.
Tel (+2712) 431 6500 or 431 6524 or 431 3060.

Consulate General in Johannesburg:
25 Cleveland, Sandhurst.

Tel (+2711)685 7540.

Consulate in Cape Town:
25 Rhodes Drive, Newlands, 8000.
Tel (+2721) 674 0579.

Consulate General in Durban:
45 Stirling Street, Durban North, 4051.
Tel (+2731) 563 4534. (National Day: 1 October)

Colombia (Republic of):
3rd Floor Park Corner Building, 1105 Park Street, Hatfield, 0083.
Tel (+2712) 342 0211/4.

Honorary Consulate in Pretoria:
77 Nondela Road, Waterkloof Heights.
Tel (+2712) 347 0126.

Honorary Consulate in Cape Town:
31 Southern Cross Drive, Constantia, 7800.
Tel (+2721) 794 3693.
(National Day: 20 July)

Comoros (The Union of):
817 Thomas Street, Corner Church and Eastwood Streets, Arcadia, 0083.
Tel (+2712) 342 0138/Mobile: (+27) 82 622 0139.
(National Day: 6 July)

Congo (Republic of):
960 Arcadia Street, Arcadia, 0007.
Tel (+2712) 342 5508.
(National Day: 15 August)

Congo (Democratic Republic of):
791 Schoeman Street, Arcadia, 0083.
Tel (+2712) 344 6475/6.

(National Day: 30 June)

Costa Rica: (Honorary Consulate):
14Taiton Road, Forest Town, Johannesburg, 2000.
Tel (+2711) 486 4716.
 (National Day: 15 September)

Cote d'Ivoire (Republic of):
795 Government Avenue, Arcadia, 0083.
 Tel (+2712)342 6913/4.
(National Day: 7 August)

Croatia (Republic of):
1160 Church Street, Colbyn, 0083.
Tel (+2712) 342 1206 /1598.
(National Day: 25 June)

Cuba (Republic of):
45 Mackenzie Street, Brooklyn, 0181.
Tel (+2712) 346 2215.
(National Day: 1 January)

Cyprus (Republic of):
Corner Hill and Church Streets, Arcadia, 0083.
Tel (+2712) 342 5258.
(National Day: 1 January)

Czech Republic:
936 Pretorius Street, Arcadia, 0083.
Tel (+2712) 431 2380 or 430 3601 or 430 2328.
(National Day: 28 October).

Denmark (Kingdom of):
Ground Floor, Block B2, Iparioli Office Park, 1166 Park Street,
Hatfield. (Pretoria).

Tel (+2712) 430 9340.

Johannesburg Honorary Consulate:
EAC Building, 19 Eastern Service Road, Eastgate extension 6, Sandton, 2199.
Tel (+2711) 804 3374 or 5. Cape Town.

Cape Town Honorary Consulate:
5 Tokai Road, Tokai, 7945.
Tel (+2721) 715 7019.

Durban Honorary Consulate:
185 Cato Road, Glenwood, 4001.
Tel (+2731) 202 9396 to 8.

Port Elizabeth Honorary Consulate:
3 Fearick Street, Korsten, Port Elizabeth, 6020.
Tel (+2741) 432 696.
(National Day: 16 April)

Djibouti (Republic of) Honorary Consulate:
138 West Street, Sandton, 2196.
Tel (+2711) 719 9111.
(National Day: 27 June)

Dominican Republic:
276 Anderson Street, Brooklyn, 0181. (Pretoria).
Tel (+2712) 362 2463.
(National Day: 27 February)

Ecuador (Republic of):
Suite 3 Selati Park, 36 Selati Street, Alphen Park. (Pretoria).
Tel (+2712) 346 1662.
(National Day: 10 August)

Egypt (Arab Republic of):
270 Bourke Street, Muckleneuk, 0002.

Tel (+2712) 343 1590 or 1.

Commercial Office:
2nd Floor Brookfield Park, 273 Middle Street, Brooklyn, 0181 (Pretoria) (+2712) 346 1654.

Press and Information Office:
Hillcrest Forum, 731 Duncan Street, Corner Lynnwood Road, Hillcrest, Pretoria.
Tel (+2712) 362 2403.
(National Day: 23 July)

Equatorial Guinea (Republic of):
48 Florence Street, Colbyn, (Pretoria).
Tel (+2712) 342 9945 or 342 6470 or 342 7087 or 342 5076.
(National Day: 12 October)

Eritrea (State of):
1281 Cobham Road, Queenswood, 0186.
Tel (+2712)333 1302.
(National Day: 24 May)

Estonia (Republic of):
15 Hofmeyer Street, Welgemoed, Bellville, 7530 (Cape Town).
Tel (+2721) 913 3850.

Gauteng office:
56 Toon van der Heever Street, Randhart, Alberton, 1457.
Tel (+27) 82 550 6363.
(National Day: 24 February)

Ethiopia (Federal Democratic Republic of):
47 Charles Street, Bailey's Muckleneuk, Brooklyn, 0181. (Pretoria)
Tel (+2712) 346 3542.
(National Day: 28 May)

European Union (Office of):

2 Green Park Estates, 27 George Storrar Drive, Groenkloof, 0181.
Tel (+2712) 452 5200.
(National Day: 9 May)

Finland (Republic of):

628 Leyds Street, Muckleneuk, 0002. (Pretoria).
Tel (+2712) 343 0275.

Commercial Office in Johannesburg:
12th Floor Sandton Office Towers, Sandton City, Sandton 2146.
Tel (+2711) 784 3164.

Embassy in Cape Town:
5 Lincoln Road, Oranjezicht, 8001.
Tel (+2721) 461 4732.

Honorary Consulate in Johannesburg:
23 Glenhove Road, Melrose Estate, 2196.
Tel (+2711) 327 5427/8/9.

Honorary Consulate in Cape Town:
85 Westlake Square, 1 Westlake Drive, Tokai, 7945.
Tel (+2721) 700 2800.
(National Day: 6 December)

France (Republic of):

250 Melk Street, Corner Middle Street, New Muckleneuk, 0181.
(Pretoria).
Tel (+2712) 425 1600.

Commercial Section:
Inanda Greens Business Park, Augusta House, 54 Wierda Road West, Wierda Valley, 2196.
Tel (+2711) 303 7150.

Johannesburg Consulate:
191 Jan Smuts Avenue, Rosebank, 2001.
Tel (+2711) 778 5600.

Cape Town Embassy:
78 Queen Victoria Street, Gardens , Cape Town, 8001.
Tel (+2721) 488 5080.

East London and Port Elizabeth Honorary Consular Agencies:
19 Currie Street, East London, 5201.
Tel (+2741) 994 6911.

Durban Honorary Consulate:
75 Columbine Place, Ring Road Industrial Park, Durban North,
4051. (Controlled by Johannesburg Consulate General)
(National Day: 14 July)

Gabon (Republic of):
921 Schoeman Street, Arcadia, 0083.
Tel (+2712) 342 4376/7.
(National Day: 17 August)

Gambia:
2nd Floor East Wing, Standard Bank Building, 11Alice Lane,
Sandton, 2196.
Tel (+2711) 884 3710.
(National Day: 18 February)

Georgia (Republic of) Honorary Consulate:
7th Floor Southern Life Centre
(+2721) 421 6355 or (+27)82 575 8888.
(National Day: 27 May)

Germany (Federal Republic of):
180 Blackwood Street, Arcadia, 0083.
Tel (+2712) 427 8900.

Legal and Consular Section in Pretoria:
1st Floor, 1267 Pretorius Street, Hatfield, 0083.
Tel (+2712) 427 8900. Visa Enquiries:

Tel (+2712) 427 8999.

Cape Town Consulate General:
19th Floor Safmarine House, 22 Riebeeck Street, Cape Town, 8001. Tel. (+2721) 405 3000.

Honorary Consulate in Durban:
4th Floor Deloitte & Touche House,
2 Devonshire Place, Durban, 4001.
Tel (+2731) 305 5677.

Honorary Consulate in Port Elizabeth:
Maritime House, 11 Uitenhage Road, North End, Port Elizabeth, 6001.
Tel (+2741) 487 2840.
(National Day: 3 October).

Ghana (Republic of):
1038 Arcadia Street, Hatfield, 0083.
Tel (+2712) 342 5847-9
(National Day: 6 March)

Greece:
1st Floor Block G, Hadefields Office Park, 1267 Church Street, Hatfield, 0083.
Tel (+2712) 430 7351/2/3.

Address during South African parliamentary session:
(Consul: K Soulios)
Reserve Bank Building, 60 St George's Mall, Cape Town, 8001.
Tel (+2721) 424 8160/1/Telex: 526474/Tel Add: GREEKONSUL.

Johannesburg Consulate:
Orbasher Place, 261 Oxford Road, Illovo.
Tel (+2711) 214 2320.

Consulate in Durban:
Suite 1101, Victoria Maine Building, 71 Victoria Embankment,

Durban, 4001.
Tel (+2731) 301 4880/1
(National/Independence Day: 25 March)

Grenada Honorary Consulate:
3rd floor Digital House, Park Lane, Sandton, 2196.
Tel (+2783) 4616559.
(National Day: 7 February)

Guatemala:
Honorary Consulate in Cape Town:
16th Floor, 2 Long Street, Cape Town, 8001.
Tel (+2721) 418 2020.

Honorary Consulate in Johannesburg:
C/O Exatrade House, Woodmead Office Park, 745 Saddle Drive,
Corner Woodmead Drive and Van Reenen Road, Woodmead,
Sandton, 2199.
Tel (+2711) 804 5080.
(National Day: 15 September)

Guinea (Republic of):
336 Orient Street, Arcadia, 0083.
Tel (+2712) 342 7348 or 342 4906.
(National Day: 2 October)

Guinea-Bissau (Republic of)
Honorary Consulate in Johannesburg:
I/F Lakeside Two, Bruma Lake, Ernest Oppenheimer Drive,
Bruma, 2198.
Tel (+2711) 622 3688.
(National Day: 24 September)

Guyana (Republic of)
Honorary Consulate in Johannesburg:

The Decision Centre, Hurlingham Manor, Sandton, 2199.
Tel (+2711) 789 9760
(National Day : 26 May)

Holy See (The Vatican)
Apostolic Nunciature in Pretoria: 4 Argo Street, Waterkloof Ridge, 0181.
Tel (+2712) 346 4235/Mobile (+2778) 333 0207.
(National Day: 19 April)

Hungary (Republic of):
959 Arcadia Street, Hatfield, 0083. (Pretoria).
Tel (+2712) 430 3020/30.

Honorary Consulate General in Cape Town:
7 Kronendal Lyn, Delsig, Stellenbosch, 7600.
Tel (+2721) 886 8855.

Honorary Consulate in Durban:
3 The Crescent East, Westway Office Park, Westville, 3629.
Tel (+2731) 251 4000.
(National Day: 20 August)

Iceland (Republic of)
Honorary Consulate General in Johannesburg (Mr MC Ramaphosa):
Tel (+2711) 305 8954.

Honorary Consulate in Cape Town:
TIR Southern Africa, 1st Floor 9 Ruby Terrace, Noordhoek, 7979.
Tel: (+2721) 789 0053/Mobile: (+2783) 253 8230.

Honorary Consulate in Durban (Dr Diliza Mji):
16 Medical Towers, 162 Old Main Road, Isipingo Rail, 4110.
Tel (+2731) 309 4126.

Honorary Consulate in Port Elizabeth:
95 Lewerkie Street, Cotswald Extension.

Tel (+2741) 364 1543.
(National Day: 17 June)

India (Republic of) High Commission:
852 Schoeman Street, Arcadia, 0083.
Tel (+2712) 342 5392/Telex: 320045-SA.

Address during parliamentary session in Cape Town:
9th Floor The Terraces, 34 Bree Street, Cape Town, 8001.
Tel (+2721) 419 8110.

Consulate General in Johannesburg:
1 Eton Road, Corner Jan Smuts Avenue and Eton Road,
Parktown, 2193.
Tel (+2711) 482 8484-8/Telex: 4-30177-SA.

Consulate General in Durban:
4th Floor Station Building, 160 Pine Street, Durban, 4001.
Tel (+2731) 304 7020-6.
(National Day: 26 January)

Indonesia (Republic of):
949 Schoeman Street, Arcadia, 0083.
Tel (+2712) 342 3350-4.

Commercial Office:
Suite 02/E4 2nd Floor Village Walk, Corner Maude and Rivonia
Road, Sandown, Sandton.
Tel (+2711) 884 6240.

Consulate General in Cape Town:
124 Rosmead Avenue, Kenilworth, Cape Town, 7708.
Tel (+2721) 761 7015.
(National Day: 17 August)

Iran (Islamic Republic of):
1002 Schoeman Street, Hatfield, 0083 (Pretoria).
Tel(+2712) 342 5880/1.

(National Day: 11 February)

Iraq (Republic of):
803 Duncan Street, Brooklyn, Pretoria, 0028.
Tel (+2712) 362 2048/9.
(National Day: 9 April).

Ireland:
1st Floor Southern Life Plaza, 1059 Schoeman Street, Corner Festival and Schoeman Streets, Arcadia, 0083.
Tel (+2712) 342 5062.

  Consulate in Cape Town:
  12th Floor LG Building, No 1 Thibault Square, Long Street, Cape Town, 8001.
  Tel (+2721) 419 0636/7.
  (National Day: 17 March)

Israel (State of):
428 King's Highway, corner of Elizabeth Grove Street and King's Highway, Lynnwood. (Pretoria)
Tel (+2712) 470 3500/1 or 470 3511 or 470 3542/3.

  Trade Office in Johannesburg:
  Marsh Building (Pty) Ltd, No 4 Sandown Valley Crescent, 3rd Floor, Sandton, 2196.
  Tel (+2711) 506 5000.
  (National Day varies annually)

Italy (Republic of):
796 George Avenue, Arcadia, 0083 (Pretoria).
Tel (+2712) 423 000.

  Cultural Office:
  165 East Avenue, Arcadia, 0083.
  Tel (+2712)343 6678.

Address during parliamentary session:
2 Grey's Pass Gardens, 8001.
(+2712) 423 5157/8.

Consulate General in Johannesburg:
37 First Avenue, (corner Second Street), Houghton, 2196.
Tel (+2711) 728 1392/3 or 728 5915.

Consulate General in Cape Town: (as for parliamentary session address above).
Tel (+2721) 487 3900.

Consulate in Durban:
1409 The Embassy, 199 Smith Street, Durban, 4001.
Tel (+2731) 368 4388/9.

Honorary Consular agencies in East London and Port Elizabeth: (controlled in Cape Town.
(National Day: 2 June)

Jamaica:
1119 Burnett Street, Hatfield, 0083.
TEL (+2712) 362 6667 Or 366 8500.
(National Day: 6 August)

Japan:
259 Baines Street, Groenkloof, 0181.
Tel. (+2712) 452 1500.
Consular section: Tel (+2712) 452 1500.

Consular Office in Cape Town:
2100 Main Tower, Standard Bank Centre, Heerengracht, 8001.
Tel (+2721) 425 1695/6.
(National Day: 23 December)

Jordan (Hashemite Kingdom of):
252 Olivier Street, Brooklyn.
Tel (+2712) 346 8615/7.

(National Day: 25 May)

Kenya (Republic of):
302 Brooks Street, Menlo Park.
Tel (+2712) 362 2249/50/51.
(National Day: 12 December)

Korea (Democratic People's Republic of):
958 Waterpoort Street, Faerie Glen. (Pretoria).
Tel (+2712) 991 8661.
(National Day: 9 September)

Korea (Republic of):
Building 3 Green Park Estates, 27 George Storrar Drive, Groenkloof, 0081.
Tel (+2712) 460 2508.

> Economic Section in Johannesburg:
> 18th Floor Sandton City Office Tower, Corner of Rivonia and 5th Streets, Sandton.
> [Tel. (+2712) 460 2509]

> Honorary Consulate General in Durban:
> 9 Fairways Park, Mount Edgecombe, 4300.
> Tel (+2731)539 2234.

> Honorary Consulate General in Cape Town:
> 7 Sunset Avenue. Landudno, Hout Bay, 7806.
> Tel (+2721) 790 9970.
> (National Day: 15 August)

Kuwait (State of):
890 Arcadia Street, Arcadia, 0083 (Pretoria).
Tel (+2712) 342 0877.
(National Day: 25 February)

Latvia (Republic of) Honorary Consulate:
The Reserve, 54 Melville Road, ILLOVO, 2196.
Tel (+2711) 750 1600.
(National Day: 18 November)

Lebanon (Republic of):
788 Government Street, Arcadia.
Tel (+2712) 430 2130.

> Honorary Consulate in Cape Town:
> No 3 "The Willows", Braeside Road, Kenilworth, 7745.
> Tel (+2721)593 5481.
> (National Day: 22 November)

Lesotho (Kingdom of):
391 Anderson Street, Menlo Park, 0081.
Tel (+2712) 460 7648.

> Consulate General in Johannesburg:
> 76 Juta Street, Indent House, Braamfontein, 2000.
> Tel (+2711) 339 3653.

> Consulate General in Durban:
> 2nd Floor Westguard House, 303 Corner West and Gardener Streets, Durban, 4001.
> Tel (+2731) 307 2168.
> (National Day:4 October)

Liberia (Republic of):
Suite 9 Section 7, Schoeman Street Forum, 1157 Schoeman Street, Hatfield.
Tel (+2712) 342 2734 or 35/Mobile (+2772) 928 0841.
Independence Day: 26 July)

Libya:
Libyan People's Bureau, 900 Church Street and Balmoral Street, Arcadia, 0083.

Tel (+2712) 342 3902.
(National Day: 1 September)

Lithuania (Republic of)

Honorary Consulate in Johannesburg:
1st Floor Killarney Mall, Riviera Road, Killarney, 2193. Tel (+2711) 486 3660.

Honorary Consulate in Cape Town:
23rd Floor, ABSA Centre, 2 Riebeeck Street, Cape Town, 8000. Tel (+2721) 421 7045.

Honorary Consulate in Pretoria:
6th Floor, 28 Church Street, Pretoria, 0002.
Tel (+2712) 328 3550.
(National Day: 16 February)

Luxembourg (Grand Duchy of):

1st Floor Fulnam House, Hampton Park, 20 Georgian Crescent, Bryanston Ext 5.
Tel (+2711) 463 1744 or 659 0961.
(National Day: 23 June)

Madagascar (Republic of):
90 B Tait Street, Colbyn.
Tel (+2712) 342 0983/4/5/6.

Consulate General in Cape Town:
4 Thelma Road, Claremont, 7708.

Consulate General in Durban:
1 Oakwood, 467 Innes Road, Morningside, 4001.
Tel (+2731) 312 9704. (National Day: 26 June)

Malawi (Republic of):

770 Government Avenue, Arcadia, 0083.
Tel (+2712) 342 0146 or 342 1759/Telex: 3 – 22017 SA.

Consulate General in Jonannesburg:

1st Floor Sable Centre House, 41 De Korte Street, Braamfontein, 2001.Tel (+2711) 339 1569.
(National Day: 6 July)

Malaysia (Federation of):
1007 Schoeman Street, Arcadia, 0083.
Tel (+2712) 342 5990/3.

Trade Office in Johannesburg:
Ground and First Floor, Building 5, Commerce Square, 39 Rivonia Road, Sandhurst.
(National Day: 31 August)

Mali (Republic of):
876 Pretorius Street, Block B, Arcadia, 0083.
Tel (+2712) 342 7464 or 342 0676.
(National Day: 22 September)

Malta Honorary Consulate in Cape Town:
332 Koeberg Road, Milnerton, 7441.
Tel (+2721) 557 7860
(National Day: 21 September)

Mauritania (Islamic Republic of):
146 Anderson Street, Brooklyn. (Pretoria)
Tel (+2712) 362 3578/Mobile: (+2776) 036 4236.
(National Day: 28 November)

Mauritius (Republic):
1163 Pretorius Street, Hatfield, 0083.
Tel (+2712) 342 1283/4.

Honorary Consulate in Durban:
11th Floor Mercury House, 320 Smith Street, Durban.
Tel (+2731) 305 1744/Mobile: (+2782) 490 0786.

Honorary Consulate in Cape Town:

Unit 2, No 1 Victoria Road, Clifton, 8005.
(National Day; 12 March)

Mexico:
Parkdev Building, Brooklyn Ridge, 570 Fehrsen Street, Brooklyn, 0181. Tel (+2712) 460 1004 or 460 0964.

Honorary Consulate in Cape Town:
2nd Floor The Spearhead Building, 42 Hans Strijdom Avenue, Foreshore, Cape Town, 8001.
Tel (+2721) 419 3848.
(National Day: 16 September)

Monaco (Principality of):
Unit 1 Milton's Way, 11 Bell Crescent Close, Westlake Business Park, Westlake, 7945 (Cape Town).
Tel (+2721) 702 0991 or 7020992.
(National Day: 19 November)

Morocco (Kingdom of):
799 Schoeman Street, Corner Farenden Street, Arcadia, 0083.
Tel (+2712) 343 0230 or 344 2340.

Honorary Consulate in Cape Town:
10 Roger Street, Valmary Park, 7550.
(National Day: 30 July)

Mozambique (Republic of):
529 Edmund Street, Arcadia, 0083.
Tel (+2712) 401 0300.

Consular Section in Pretoria:
75 Hamilton Street, Arcadia, 0083.
Tel (+2712)321 2288.

Consulate General in Johannesburg:
131 Oxford Road, Illovo.

Tel (+2711) 336 1819 or 21 or 24 or27 or 28 or 336 9921.

Consulate in Cape Town:
7th Floor, 45 Castle Street, Cape Town, 8001.
Tel (+2721) 462 2944/5.

Consulate in Durban:
Room 520 5th Floor, 320 West Street, Durban ,4001.
Tel (+2731) 304 0200.

Consulate in Nelspruit:
43 Brown Street, Nelspruit, 1201.
Tel (+2713) 752 7396, (National Day: 25 June)

Myanmar (The Union of):
201 Leyds Street, Arcadia, 0083.
Tel (+2712) 341 2556/7.
(National Day: 4 January)

Namibia (Republic of):
197 Blackwood Street, Arcadia, 0083.
Tel (+2712) 481 9100.

Consulate General in Cape Town:
3 Newlands Roads, Claremont. Tel (+2721).
(National Day: 21 March)

Nepal (Federal Democratic Republic of):
453 Fehrsen Street, Bailey's Muckleneuk, Brooklyn. (Pretoria).
Tel (+2712) 346 2399.
(National Day: 7 July)

Netherlands:
201 Queen Wilhemina Avenue, Nieuw Muckleneuk. (Pretoria).
Tel (+2712) 425 4500.

Consulate General in Cape Town:

100 Strand Street, Cape Town, 8001.
Tel (+2721) 421 5660-3.

Honorary Consulate in Durban:
8th Floor Standard Bank Centre, 135 Musgrave Road, Durban
4001.
Tel (+2731) 202 0461.
(National Day: 30 April)

New Zealand:
125 Middle Street, Muckleneuk, 0181.
Tel (+2712) 435 9000.

Honorary Consulate in Cape Town: 345 Lansdowne Road,
Corner Denver Road and Lansdowne Road, Cape Town, 7700.
Tel (+2721) 696 8561.
(National Day: 6 February)

Nigeria (Federal Republic of):
971 Schoeman Street, Arcadia, 0083.
Tel (+2712) 342 0805/0663/0668/0642/0947/0934.

Consulate General in Johannesburg:
16 Rivonia Road, Illovo.
Tel (+2711) 442 3620.
(National Day: 1 October)

Norway (Kingdom of):
A2 Iparioli Building, 1166 Park Street, Hatfield, 0083.
Tel (+2712) 342 6100.

Commercial Office in Johannesburg:
14th Floor Office Towers, Sandton City, Sandton.
Tel (+2711) 784 8150.

Address during parliamentary session:
17th Floor Southern Life Centre, 8 Riebeeck Street, Cape Town,
8001.

Tel (+2721) 425 1687.

Honorary Consulate in Cape Town:
28th Floor 2805 ABSA Building, 2 Riebeeck Street, Cape Town, 8001.
Tel (+2721) 418 1276.

Honorary Consulate in Durban:
17 Overport Drive, Berea, Durban, 4001.
Tel (+2731) 207 6900.
(Constitution Day: 17 May)

Oman (Sultanate of):
11 Anderson Street, Brooklyn.
Tel (+2712) 362 8301 or 362 2766 or 362 3114.
(National Day: 18 November)

Pakistan (Islamic Republic of):
263 Orion Avenue, Waterkloof Ridge. (Pretoria).
Tel (+2712) 362 4072 or 3 or 362 3967/ Telex 320006HICOP

SA.Commercial Office:
100 Sandton Drive, Parkmore, 2196.
Tel (+2711) 880 8673/4.
(National Day:23 March)

Palestine (State of):
809 Government Avenue, Arcadia, 0083.
Tel (+2712) 342 6411.
(National Day: 29 November)

Panama (Republic of):
239 Kloof Avenue, Waterkloof Ridge, 0181. (Pretoria).
Tel (+2712) 346 7034/0703.

Honorary Consulate in Durban:
26th Floor Old Mutual Centre, 303 West Street, Durban, 4001.

Tel (+2731) 336 2682/Mobile: (+2772) 994 4332.
(National Day: 3 November)

Paraguay (Republic of):
189 Strelitzia Road, Waterkloof Heights, 0181. (Pretoria)
Tel (+2712) 347 1047 or 8).
(National Day: 15 May)

Peru (Republic of):
200 Saint Patrick Street, Muckleneuk Hill, 0083 (Pretoria).
Tel (+2712) 440 1030 or 1. (National Day: 28 July)

Phillipines (Republic of):
54 Nicholson Street, Muckleneuk. (Pretoria).
Tel (+2712) 346 0451 or 2.

Honorary Cape Town Consulate:
85 Main Road, Muizenberg, 7945.
(+2721) 788 9265).
(National Day: 12 June)

Poland (Republic of):
14 Amos Street, Colbyn, 0083.
Tel (+2712) 430 2631 or 2.

Commercial Section:
56 Sixth Street, Houghton, 2198. (Johannesburg).
Tel (+2711) 788 6597.
(National Day: 11 November)

Portugal (Republic of):
599 Leyds Street, Muckleneuk, 0002. (Pretoria).
(+2712) 341 2340/1/2.

Commercial office in Johannesburg:
Suite 224, Killarney Mall, Killarney.
Tel (+2711) 486 0256/58.

Consular Section:
Suite 03 Ground Floor, Groenkloof Forum Office Park, 57 George Storrar Drive, Groenkloof, 0181.
Tel (+2712) 341 5522.

Address during parliamentary session in Cape Town:
1006 Main Tower, Standard Bank Centre, Hertzog Boulevard, Cape Town, 8001.
Tel (+2721) 214 560 – 2 or (+2721) 418 0080/1.

Consulate in Johannesburg:
1st Floor Portuguese House, Ernest Oppenheimer Avenue, Bruma, 2198. Tel (+2711)622 0645 - 9

Consulate in Durban:
Suite 1612 16th Floor, 320 West Street, Durban, 4001.
Tel (+2731) 305 7511.
(National Day: 10 June)

Qatar (State of):
355 Charles Street, Waterkloof, 0181. (Pretoria).
Tel (+2712) 452 1700.
(National Day: 3 September)

Romania (Republic of):
117 Charles Street, Brooklyn, 0181.
Tel (+2712) 460 6940.

Consulate General in Cape Town:
"Helderberg", 53 Herschel Road, Kenilworth, 7700.
Tel (+2721) 761 1781.
(National Day: 1 December)

Russian Federation:
316 Brooks Street, Menlo Park, 0081.
Tel (+2712) 362 1337/8 or 362 7116.

Consulate General in Cape Town:
2nd Floor, Southern Life Centre, 8 Riebeeck Street, Cape Town, 8001.
Tel (+2721) 418 3656/57.
(National Day: 12 June)

Rwanda (Republic of):
983 Schoeman Street, Arcadia, 0083.
Tel (+2712) 342 6536. (National Day: 4 July)

Sahrawi Arab Democratic Republic:
801 Merton Avenue, Arcadia, 0083.
Tel (+2712) 342 5532.
(National Day: 27 February)

San Marino (Republic of):
Honorary Consulate in Pretoria: No address.
Tel (+2712) 460 5826.
(Honorary Consul General: EA Loubser)
(National Day: 3 September)

Saudi Arabia (Kingdom of):
711 Duncan Street/corner Lunnon Street, Brooklyn/Hatfield).
Tel (+2712) 362 4230 or 362 4240.

Religious Office:
146A Percy Street, Eastwood, 0001. (Pretoria).
Tel (+2712) 342 4011.

Senegal (Republic of):
Charles Manor, 57 Charles Street, Bailey's Muckleneuk, 0181.
Tel (+2712) 460 5263.

Honorary Consulate in Johannesburg:
91 Central Street, Houghton.
Tel (+2711) 483 0889

(National Day: 4 April)

Serbia (Republic of):
163 Marais Street, Brooklyn.
Tel (+2712) 460 5626 or 460 6103.
(National Day: 15 February)

Seychelles (Republic of):
296 Glenwood Road, Lynnwood Park, 0181.
Tel (+2712) 348 0270.

> Consulate General in Johannesburg:
> 81 William Nicol Drive, Bryanston, Sandton.
> Tel (+2772) 259 6132.
> (National Day: 18 June)

Singapore (Republic of):
980 – 982 Schoeman Street, Arcadia, 0083.
 Tel (+2712) 430 6035.
(National Day: 9 August)

Slovak (Republic of):
930 Arcadia Street, Arcadia, 0083.
Tel (+2712) 342 2051 or 2.
(National Day: 1 September)

Slovenia (Republic of):
Honorary Consulate in Cape Town: Plexus House, 9 Queen Street,
Durbanville, 7551.
Tel (+2721) 970 2447.
(National Day: 25 June)

Spain (Republic of):
Lord Charles Building, 337 Brooklyn Road, Brooklyn.
Tel (+2712) 460 0123.

Commercial Office in Johannesburg:
8th Floor Norwich Life Towers, Fredman Drive, Corner Bute
Lane, Sandton, 2196.
Tel (+2711) 883 2102.

Address during parliamentary session in Cape Town:
37 Shortmarket Street, Cape Town.
(+2721) 422 2326 or 7 or 422 2415.

Honorary Consulate in Johannesburg:
7 Coronation Street, Sandhurst, 2196.
Tel (+2711) 783 2046.

Honorary Consulate in Durban:
120 Abrey Road, Kloof, 3610.
Tel (+2731) 764 2574.
(National Day: 12 October)

Sri Lanka (Democratic Socialist Republic of):
410 Alexander Street, Broooklyn, 0181 (Pretoria).
Tel (+2712) 460 7690 or 460 7679.

Honorary Consulate in Cape Town: 15 Piet Retief Street,
Stellenbosch, 7600. (+2721) 887 8018.
(National Day: 4 February)

Sudan (Republic of the):
1203 Pretorius Street, Hatfield, 0083.
Tel (+2712) 342 4538 or 342 7903.
(National Day: 1 January)

Suriname (Republic of):
Suite no 4 Groenkloof Forum Office Park, 57 George Storrar
Drive, Groenkloof, 0181.
Tel (+2712) 346 7627/45.
(National Day: 25 November)

Swaziland (Kingdom of):

iParioli Complex, 1166 Park Street, Hatfield, 0083.
Tel (+2712) 426 6400.

Commercial Office in Johannesburg:
Swedish Trade Council, Ground Floor, Oakhill Building.
Fourways Golf Park, Roos Street, Fourways.
Tel (+2711) 300 5600.

Honorary Consulate in Cape Town:
2805 ABSA Building, 2 Riebeeck Building, Cape Town.
Tel (+2721) 418 1276. (National Day: 6 June)

Switzerland:

225 Veale Street, Parc Nouveau, New Muckleneuk, 0181.
Tel 9+2712) 452 0660.

Address during parliamentary session in Cape Town:
26th Floor, 1 Thibault Square, corner Long and Hans Strijdom
Streets, Cape Town, 8001.
Tel (+2721) 418 3669.

Swiss Agency for Development and Cooperation in Pretoria:
Unit 4 Parkfield Court, 1185 Park Street, Hatfield, 0083.
Tel (+2712) 362 2972.

Honorary Consulate in Durban:
216 Cozumel, 33 North Beach Road, Umdloti Beach, 4350.
Tel (+2731) 568 2457.
(National Day: 1 August)

Syrian Arab Republic:

963 Schoeman Street, Arcadia, 0083.
Tel. (+2712) 342 4701 or 342 4566.
(National Day: 17 April)

Taiwan:

1147 Schoeman Street, Hatfield, 0083 (Pretoria).

Tel (+2712) 430 6071 – 3.

Address during parliamentary session in Cape Town:
10th Floor Main Tower, Standard Bank Centre, Foreshore, 8001.
Tel (+2721) 418 1188.

Office of the Economic Division in Johannesburg:
2nd Floor North, Cradock Place, 5 Cradock Avenue, Rosebank,
2196.
Tel (+2711) 442 8880/1.

Office of the Information Division in Johannesburg: Ground
Floor Block 3, Albury Office Park, Magalieszicht Avenue,
Dunkeld West, 2196.
Tel (+2711) 325 4613 or 325 6101.

Taipei Liason Office in Johannesburg.
14th Floor North, Sandton City Office Tower, Corner Rivonia
Road and 5th Street, Sandton.
(National Day: 10 October).

Tanzania (United Republic of):
822 George Avenue, Arcadia, 0083.
Tel (+2712) 342 4371 or 342 4393.
(Union Day: 26 April)

Thailand (Kingdom of):
428 Hill Street, Corner Hill and Pretorius Streets, Arcadia, 0083.
Tel (+2712) 342 5470 or 342 4516 or 342 4506.

Commercial Office in Pretoria: (As above).
Tel (+2712) 342 0835 or 342 0850 or 342 0856.
(National Day: 5 December)

Trinidad and Tobago (Republic of):
258 Lawley Street, Waterkloof, Pretoria.
Tel (+2712) 460 9688.

Honorary Consulate in Johannesburg:

305 Kambula Apts, Corner Alice Lane and Fifth Streets, Sandton, 2146.

Tel. (+2711) 883 0087 or 883 9631 or 884 3808/Telex: 521691 STREX SA.

(National Day: 31 August)

Tunisia (Republic of):

850 Church Street, Arcadia, 0083.

Tel (+2712) 342 6282or 83/ Telex 320053 TUEMB SA.

Honorary Consulate in Cape Town:
40 Fifth Avenue, Rondebosch East.
Tel (+2721) 697 0293.
(National Day: March)

Turkey (Republic of):

1067 Church Street, Hatfield, 0028.

Tel (+2712) 342 6055 or 53 or 54 (Visa section), Tel (+2712) 342 6051 (Commercial Office).

Honorary Consulate in Cape Town:
Old Post Office, Main Road, St James, 7945.
Tel (+2721) 788 7069. (National Day: 29 October)

Uganda (Republic of):

882 Church Street, Arcadia, 0083.
Tel (+2712) 342 6031/3.
(National Day: 9 October)

Ukraine:

398 Marais Street, Brooklyn, 0181.
Tel (+2712) 460 1946.
(National Day: 24 August)

United Arab Emirates:

992 Arcadia Street, Arcadia. (Pretoria).

Tel (+2712) 342 7736.
(National Day: 2 December)

United Kingdom of Great Britain and Northern Ireland:
Her Britannic Majesty's High Commission: "Greystoke", 255 Hill
Street, Arcadia, 0083.
Tel (+2712)   421 7500.

Cultural Section:
Suite 1, Sanlam Gables, 1209 Schoeman Street, Hatfield, 0083.
(+2712) 431 2400.

Consular Section in Pretoria:
Block B 1st Floor, Liberty Life Place, 256 Glyn Street, Hatfield,
0083.
Tel (+2712) 483 1400.

Her Britannic Majesty's High Commission in Cape Town:
91 Parliament Street, Cape Town, 8001.
Tel (+2721) 461 7220.

Department for International Development in Pretoria:
2nd Floor Sanlam Building, 353 Festival Street, Hatfield, 0083.
Tel (+2712) 431 2100.

Commercial Office in Johannesburg:
Dunkeld Corner, 275 Jan Smuts Avenue, Dunkeld West, 2196.
Tel (+2711) 537 7000 or (+2711) 327 0163 (Information
Section).

Consulate General in Cape Town:
Southern Life Centre, 8 Riebeeck Street, Cape Town, 8000.
Tel (+2721) 425 3670.

Commercial Office in Durban:
19th Floor The Marine, 22 Gardiner Street, 4001.
Tel (+2731) 305 3041.

Honorary Consulate for British Cultural and Heritage
Association, FWJK Court, 86 Armstrong Road, La Lucia Ridge,

Durban, 4000.
Tel (+2731) 572 7259.

Honorary Consulate in Port Elizabeth:
First Bowring House, 66 Ring Road, Greenacres, Port Elizabeth, 6001.
Tel (+2741) 363 8841.
(National Day: 9 June)

United States of America:
877 Pretorius Street, Arcadia, 0083.
Tel (+2712) 431 4000/(after hours) (+2782) 285 2341.

Consulate General in Johannesburg:
1 Sandton Drive, Sandhurst, 2196.
Tel (+2711) 290 3000.

United States Information Service in Johannesburg:
3rd Floor 1066 Building, Corner Pritchard and Harrison Street, Johannesburg, 2001.
Tel (+2711) 838 2231.

Consulate General in Cape Town:
4th Floor Broadway Industries Centre, Foreshore, Cape Town, 8001.
Tel (+2721) 421 4280 – 3.

United States Information Service in Cape Town:
7th Floor Broadway Building, Hertzog Boulevard, Foreshore, Cape Town, 8001.
Tel (+2721) 461 0583 – 5.

Consulate General in Durban:
29th Floor Durban Bay House, 333 Smith Street, Durban, 4001.
Tel (+2731) 304 4737.

United States Agency for International Development in Pretoria:
100 Totius Street, Groenkloof X5.
Tel (+2712) 452 2000.

(National Day: 4 July)

Uruguay:
3rd Floor 1119 Burnett Street, Glenrand MIB House, Hatfield, 0083.
Tel (+2712) 362 6521/22.
(National Day: 25 August)

Vanuatu (Republic of):
1 Grosvenor Court, High Level Road 78, Green Point, 8002.
(Cape Town).
Tel (+2721) 434 6570.
(National Day: 30 July).

Venezuela (Bolivarian Republic of):
1st Floor Suite 4, Hatfield Gables South , 474 Hilda Street, Hatfield, 0083.
Tel (+2712) 362 6592 or 3 or 4.
(Independence Day: 5 July)

Vietnam (Socialist Republic of):
87 Brook Street, Brooklyn, 0181.
Tel (+2712) 362 8119.
(National Day: 2 September)

Yemen (Republic of):
329 Main Street, Waterkloof, 0181.
Tel (+2712) 425 0760.
(National Day: 22 May).

Zambia (Republic of):
Zambia House, 570 Ziervoel Avenue, Arcadia, 0083.
Tel (+2712) 326 1854.
(National Day: 24 October)

Zimbabwe (Republic of):

Zimbabwe House: 798 Merton Street, Arcadia, 0083.
Tel (+2712) 342 5125/Telex: 320055ZIMPA SA.

Consulate General in Johannesburg:
17th Floor, 20 Anderson Street, Johannesburg, 2001.
Tel (+2711) 838 2156/7/8/9
(National Day: 18 April)

The following countries currently do not have diplomatic representation in South Africa:

1. Afghanistan
2. Andorra
3. Antigua and Barbuda
4. Armenia
5. Azerbaijan
6. Bahamas
7. Bahrain
8. Barbados
9. Belize
10. Bhutan
11. Bosnia and Herzegovina
12. Brunei Darussalam
13. Cambodia
14. Cape Verde
15. Cook Islands
16. Commonwealth of Dominica
17. East Timor/Timor Leste
18. El Salvador
19. Fiji
20. (Former Republic of Yugoslavia) Macedonia

21. Haiti
22. Honduras
23. Kiribati
24. Kyrgyz Republic
25. Lao People's Democratic Republic
26. Liechtenstein
27. Marshall Islands
28. Micronesia
29. Mongolia
30. Moldova
31. Nauru
32. Nicaragua
33. Niger
34. Palau
35. Papua New Guinea
36. Saint Kitts and Nevis
37. Saint Lucia
38. Saint Vincent and the Grenadines
39. Samoa
40. Sierra Leone
41. Solomon Islands
42. Somalia
43. Tajikistan
44. Togo
45. Tonga Kingdom
46. Turkmenistan
47. Tuvalu
48. Uzbekistan

INTERNATIONAL ORGANIZATIONS REPRESENTED IN SOUTH AFRICA

African Development Bank:
Block B Crestway, 3 Hotel Street, Persequor Park, Lynnwood, 0020.
Tel (+2712) 818 6900 or 818 7200 or 349 5207/8/9/10/Mobile:
(+2779) 019 8513.

Africa Institute for Environmentally Sound Management of Hazardous and other Wastes:
9th Floor South Tower, 315 Pretorius Street, Fedsure Forum Building, Pretoria, 0001.
Tel (+2712) 310 3627.

European Investment Bank (Southern Africa and Indian Ocean Regional Representation:
5 Green Park Estates, 27 George Storrar Drive, Groenkloof, Pretoria, 0181.
Tel (+2712) 425 0460.

Food, Agriculture and Natural Resources Policy Analysis Network:
141 Cresswell Road, Weavind Park, Silverton. (Pretoria).
International Committee of the Red Cross (ICRC): 794 Church Street, Arcadia. (Pretoria). Tel (+2712) 430 7335/6/7

International Centre for Genetic Engineering and Biotechnology (Institute for Infectious Diseases and Molecular Medicine):
Level 1 and 2 Werner & Beit Building (South), Anzio Road, Observatory, 7925. (Cape Town).
Tel (+2721) 650 7687.

International Finance Corporation IFC Sub-Saharan Hub):
14 Fricke Road, Illovo, 2196 (Johannesburg).
Tel (+2711) 731 3000.Cape Town Office: 13th Floor Thibault

Square, Long Street, Cape Town, 8001.
Tel (+2721) 418 7177/9

International Institute for Democracy and Electoral Assistance (IDEA):
337 Brooklyn Drive, Lord Charles Office Park, Brooklyn (Pretoria).
Tel (+2712) 460 5305/Mobile: (+2783) 266 8274.

International Labour Organization (ILO):
347 Hilda Street, Hatfiled, 0083.
Tel (+2712) 431 8800

International Monetary Fund (IMF):
1st Floor Building B2, 1166 Park Street, Hatfield, 0001.
Tel (+2712) 342 3444/3457.

International Organization for Migration (IOM):
826 Government Avenue, Arcadia, 0083.
Tel (+2712) 342 1961 or 342 2789.

International Federation of the Red Cross and Red Crescent Societies (IFRC):
44 Wierda Road West, Wierda Valley, Sandton, 2196. (Johannesburg).
Tel (+2711) 303 9700.

International Water Management Institute IWMI):
Block D9/, 141 Cresswell Road, Silverton. (Pretoria).
Tel (+2712) 845 9100.

The New Partnership for Africa's Development NEPAD):
Gateway Park B, International Business Gateway, Corner Challenger and Colombia Avenue, Midridge Office Park, Midrand, 1685.
Tel (+2711) 256 3600.

The Regional Tourism Organization of Southern Africa (RETOSA):

Waterfall Park, Corner MacMac Road and Howic Close, Waterfall Park, Midrand.
Tel (+2711) 315 2420/1

United Nations Food and Agriculture Organization in South Africa:
6th Floor Metropark Building, 351 Corner Schoeman and Prinsloo Streets, Pretoria, 0002.
Tel (+2712) 354 8000

United Nations High Commissioner for Refugees (UNHCR):
8th Floor, Metropark Building, 351 Corner Schoeman and Prinsloo Streets, Pretoria, 0002.
Tel (+2712) 354 8303.

United Nations Industrial Development Organization (UNIDO): The DTI Campus, 77 Meintjies Street, Pretoria, 0002.
Tel (+2712) 394 5463

United Nations International Children's Emergency Fund (UNICEF):
6th Floor Metropark Building, 351 Schoeman Street, Pretoria, 0001Tel (+2712) 342 8200

United Nations Development Programme (UNDP):
9th and 10th Floors Metropark Building, 351 Schoeman Street, Pretoria, 0001.
Tel (+2712) 354 8000.

United Nations Information Centre:
6th floor Metropark Building, 351 Schoeman Street, Pretoria, 0001.
Tel (+2712) 354 8500

United Nations Office for the Coordination of Humanitarian Affairs OCHA):

Idion House, 14 Naivasha Road, Sunninghill, 2157 (Johannesburg).
Tel (+2711) 517 1594

United Nations Office on Drugs and Crime (UNODC):
2nd Floor Southern Life Plaza, 1059 Schoeman Street, Hatfield, 0028 (Pretoria).
Tel (+2712) 342 2424

United Nations Office of Project Services (UNOPS):
7 Kikuyu Road, Sunninghill, 2052. (Johannesburg).
Tel (+2711) 259 6570.

United Nations Population Fund:
5th Floor Metropark Building, 351 Schoeman Street, corner Prinsloo Streets, Pretoria, 0001.
Tel (+2712) 354 8401.

Johannesburg office: 7 Naivasha Road, Sunninghill, 2157.
Tel (+2711) 603 5100

World Bank:
442 Rodericks Road, Lynnwood, 0081.
Tel (+2712) 348 8895.

World Food Programme (WFP):
Idion Building, 11 Naivasha Road, Sunninghill, 2157.
Tel (+2711) 517 1634.

World Health Organization (WHO):
Metropark Building, 351 Schoeman Street, Pretoria, 0002.
Tel (+2712) 354 8556

Chapter Five

EMERGENCIES AND EVACUATION SERVICES

Unexpected and unplanned for occurrences invariably prove costly, as they result in bodily injury, deterioration of chronic health problems (like Systemic Hypertension and Diabetes Mellitus) and missed flights. In the past five years tourists have been unwitting passengers who got injured in bus crashes in countries as diverse as Peru, India and South Africa. Rented cars can suffer from electrical faults. They can be hijacked/carjacked and passengers may end up harmed. In this section we present sources of help when such eventualities disrupt one's travel itinerary in South Africa and her neighbours.

LAW AND ORDER/POLICE SERVICES

LESOTHO

(LMPS)

Crime STOP : +266 22317262 and +266 58881011 or 2 or 3 or 4 or 5.

BOTSWANA

Emergency number 999 and 39 14948

Towing and low bed services

Insofar as these services are concerned some companies like Van Wettens, MOZHELP and the Automobile Association of South Africa (the "AA") are active cross-border.

Van Wettens offers emergency towing services as well as low bed carrier services for extremely larger items that have to be transported by road. Their toll free number is (+27) 800-115200

-The "AA" also offers towing services in Southern Africa. In South Africa they operate Road Patrols and they also have their own fleet of suitable trucks, manned by trained mechanics. In cases where it's not feasible to send their own car to the scene of car failure, they have a network of contracted operators who customer help reaches the stranded motorist soonest. The "AA" has a reciprocal membership of the Federation Internationale de l'Automobile (FIA), the governing body for world motorsport and a federation of the world's leading Touring Clubs and Automobile Associations. It is active and represented in 130 countries.

To check reciprocal benefits of the country you intend visiting go to http://www.fiatraveller.com/globalservice.php. (You'll need a username and a password for access…)

The "AA" also offers South African road condition information, free telephonic motoring related legal advice, route planning, toll information, distances, and directions-during office hours- in English via telephone, facsimile or email from their travel information centre.

Emergency numbers for the "AA" are: +27-83-843 22 or +27-800 111 998 or +27-11-799 1670 or +27-11-799 1400

Cross-border documentation can be arranged telephonically, by facsimile or email through the "AA"s Foreign Travel department at:

Telephone: +27-11-799 10 40 or 41 or 42
Facsimile: +27-11-799 10 41
Email: jchabedi@aasa.co.za or opombo@aasaa.co.za

MOZHELP is an integrated entity offering professional service providers who interact to provide emergency medical services, business management assistance in compliance with Mozambican laws, lawyers, doctors, roadside and security assistance services. Like the "AA" breakdown assistance is provided by approved local service providers.

Their contact details are:

Telephone: +27-11-794 5614
Facsimile: +27-86-689 7335
Email: mozaccm@netactive.co.za

Related services

OUTSURANCE-over and above standard car insurance-offers OUT-in-Africa insurance cover for 4X4/SUVs, trailers, motorcycles, caravans and watercraft against loss or damage even for full off-road use as per manufacturer's specifications. This unique offering extends beyond SACU member countries and includes Angola, Kenya, Tanzania, Uganda and Zambia.

Rental companies

All car rental companies operational in South African points of entry offer comprehensive short-term car and third party insurance and advice on what to do in a motoring emergency.

Credit card providers

These divisions of financial institutions offer incentivised travel insurance packages to the different types of clients they have.

The Four Wheel Drive Club of South Africa

This club-over and above emergency assistance in the event of an accident, mechanical or electrical breakdown-offers comprehensive 4X4 Vehicle Insurance including an extensive range of leisure and travel equipment for travel in all SACU member countries as well as further afield, for instance, Angola, Malawi, Zambia, Kenya and Uganda. This package also includes 911 Medical Rescue.

Contact details are:

Telephone:	+27-11-789 7845
Facsimile:	+27-11-789 2507
Mobile:	+27-82- 568 8518
Email:	peter@genesisib.co.za

ZIMBABWE

Automobile Association Zimbabwe (AA Zimbabwe):
Tel +263 4 752 779
(24 hour roadside assistance): +263 4 707 959.

Road Angels:
(+263 772) 122122 or (+263 4) 334418

Road Rescue Recovery 24hour technical assistance:
(+263 773) 300800 or 133000

www.aasa.co.za
www.assist247.co.za

Emergency Medical Services

Private medical facilities and care in South Africa compares favourably with the best all over world. Its excellent transport infrastructure ensures easy access to private medical facilities countrywide. However, the same unfortunately cannot be said of private medical facilities in countries neighbouring South Africa, hence the need to prepare oneself for early evacuation to South Africa for urgent medical intervention. To this end several products are now available to evacuate stricken travellers to medical facilities they may be accustomed to in their home countries.

It is our assumption that not all travellers purchase comprehensive travel insurance. By "comprehensive" we mean insurance that will-were one to be incapacitated by sudden illness or injury-immediately pay for all necessary, safe and quick transportation (by air or road) to the nearest South African medical institution. It should be able to pay for further treatment and care of the stricken traveller in the event of there being a real need for further treatment and/or rehabilitation in the traveller's home country or another country whose medical specialists offer rare expertise. Such transport should always have world class medical resuscitation equipment and appropriately trained personnel. Such facilities should be of such a nature that the stricken traveller can-within reasonable limits-be returned to one's previous level of health, and be strong enough to resume one's journey.

As far as state medical services are concerned we have included details of hospitals or clinics that ca offer a wider range of services, akin to those offered at private medical institutions.

In this section providers of care have incorporated different but interrelated products aimed at easy the stricken traveller's health-seeking burden. Such products include the following critical services:

1. Security assistance including threat assessment and personnel protection including mobile armed protection.
2. Emergency medical assistance including 24 hour immediate paramedic response, intensive care transportation and evacuation service by fixed or rotor wing aircraft.
3. Associated Insurance Brokers (AIB) offers integrated products including comprehensive travel insurance and are associated with several international entities that have an excellent record in the executive travel industry like Europ Assistance Worldwide Services SA, Chartis South Africa, Matrix Vehicle Tracking and Fidelity Guarantee Acceptances.

BOTSWANA

In the capital city of Gaborone three private hospitals exist, namely Bokamoso (telephone number: 369 4000); Gaborone (telephone number: 3901999) and Princess Marina (telephone: 3953221)

LESOTHO

ER24 084 124 offers emergency paramedical services and works in conjunction with Ladybrand Medi-Clinic Day hospital for-amongst others-stricken travellers within Lesotho.

Execuline in Lesotho offers Roadside assistance-linked car hire, personal accident cover and third party liability cover. Travel insurance is also offered.

Hotline: 0860 10 34 34

MOZAMBIQUE

Mozhelp offers professional service providers in the fields of Emergency Medicine, Law, Roadside and Security Assistance services. Contact details are:

Telephone: +27-11-794 5614
Facsimile: +27-86-689 7335
Email: mozaccm@netactive.co.za

1. Central Hospital de Maputo is located on a square bounded by Agostinho Neto Avenida, Avenida Eduardo Mondlane, Avenida Tomas Nduda and Avenida Salvador Allende. Access route and bearings: From Ressano Garcia border post travel on the EN4. Turn left into EN1 which takes you straight into Maputo City. Beyond the circle as you enter the city, EN1 becomes Avenida 24 de Julho. Turn left intoAvenida Avenida Salvador Allende. Tel. (+258) 21 496 444 or 21320828
2. Hospital Geral do Chamanculo. Tel (+25821) 400086
3. Hospital Geral Jose Macamo, Maputo. Tel (+25821) 400177

4. Hospital Geral de Mavalane: Avenida das FPLM, Maputo. Tel/Fax (+25821) 460416.

5. Hospital Gerald a Machava: Rua do Jardim, Machava. Tel(+25821) 708144/5

6. Hospital Psiquiatrico do Infulene: Avenida de Mocambique 6.5km on the EN4 to Xai Xai (Psychiatric Hospital): Tel (+25821) 470623.

7. Hospital Militar do Maputo: Avenida Olof Palme, Maputo. Tel ((+25821) 400112

(See http://maputo.usembassy.gov/uploads/images for Healthcare options in Mozambique)

NAMIBIA

Medical services in Namibia are of a very high standard, but availability is restricted. In the capital city of Windhoek medical facilities are adequate and well-equipped, as are those of outlying towns-though the range of services may vary.

Contact details

Outside Windhoek the dialling code is 061 and precedes the Windhoek telephone number. From South Africa all the following numbers should be preceded by +26461 or 0026461. For instance, you will go through to Medi-Clinic Windhoek when you ring +26461222687 or 0026461222687.

Aeromed   249 777 or 230 505
MedRescue   230 505/6/7

Hospitals

Medi-Clinic Windhoek	Tel (+264 61) 222 687
	(www.mediclinic.co.za)
Windhoek Central Hospital	Tel (+264 61) 203 9111
Katutura Hospital	Tel (+264 61) 203 9111
Roman Catholic Hospital	Tel (+264 61) 237 237

Rhino Park Private Hospital
(Day Care clinic only with no emergency unit).
Khomas Medical Services: Tel 225 434
4758 Swarts Avenue, Khomasdal.
Tel (+264 61) 213 424

Prosperity Health (www.prosperityhealth.com) offers an integrated product menu including emergency evacuation, medical and hospital network provider services in the whole of Africa. They have eight sites in Namibia:

Windhoek
Corner Field & Thorer Streets
+264 61 299 9000

Walvis Bay Medical Park
Hidepo Hamutenya Street
+264 64 206 098/118

Tsumeb Safari Centre,
Omagalle Street
+264 67 222 975/924
Oranjemund
Cnr 8th avenue & 12th Street
+264 63 232 295

Luderitz
Block D 02nd floor, Waterfront

+264 63 202 143
Oshakati
No. 7 The Palms, Cnr Robert Mugabe & Main Rd
+264 65 222 335/ 395
Swakopmund
Werf street Nr 5
+264 64 461356

Rosh Pinah
Lood Street, SPAR Centre No 5
+264 63 274958

SWAZILAND

Medical Emergency Traumalink
7606 0911

Alliance International Medical Services for Emergency Evacuation
+27-11-83 2287804 or +27-11-82 323 7553 (24hours)
+27-11- 783 0135 (24hours)

To assist individual travellers' unique problems, AIMS requires your medical doctor to email them your medical details in order to be ready to help at short notice and also to provide a cost estimate. Their bouquet of services includes hospital admission in specialist centres of "excellence", medical updates/daily visits, account administration and cost containment, Air Ambulance (emergency evacuation), visa requirements/ground transport, translators, step-down facilities and family accommodation.

SWAZILAND

Manzini Clinic   25057430
Mbabane Clinic   2404 2423 (24hour trauma care and lab)
Good Shepherd Hospital, Siteki. 2343 4133

ZIMBABWE

ER24

Netcare 911   082 911 in RSA (
Reverse charge calls are accepted in Jhb over 24hours.
+27-11-254 1392

Prosperity Health (www.prosperityhealth.com) offers an integrated product menu including emergency evacuation, medical and hospital network provider services in the whole of Africa. They have eight sites in Namibia:

Windhoek
Corner Field & Thorer Streets
+264 61 299 9000

Walvis Bay Medical Park
Hidepo Hamutenya Street
+264 64 206 098/118

Tsumeb Safari Centre
Omagalle Street
+264 67 222 975/924

Oranjemund
Cnr 8th avenue & 12th Street
 +264 63 232 295

Luderitz
Block D 02nd floor, Waterfront
+264 63 202 143

Oshakati
No. 7 The Palms, Cnr Robert Mugabe & Main Rd

+264 65 222 335/ 395

Swakopmund
Werf street Nr 5
 +264 64 461356

Rosh Pinah
Lood Street, SPAR Centre No 5
+264 63 274958

ZIMBABWE

Prosperity Health

For emergency evacuation in Zimbabwe contact Wendy Hulbert on +263 04 746232 or 04 746227; Cel/fax +263 04 091253175

Chapter Six

FORENSIC/PATHOLOGY SERVICES

Commonly post-mortems are done at Pathology section of a tertiary level hospital (attached to a medical school). These hospitals are often situated centrally in the capital cities of each respective country. Where there's a fee chargable, that fee is often nominal. Private forensic pathologists also perform post-mortems where people have died under suspicious/unnatural circumstances overseas.

Further, burial companies often have easier and quicker access to forensic post-mortem services whenever needed.

Exhumation of mortal remains and follow up forensic post-mortems are done in conjunction with the respective courts of law assisted by the police services of each country.

BOTSWANA

Gaborone Government Hospital
Funeral Services Group (FSG) Botswana
Tel. +267 392 2074 or +267 3696200 (call centre)/Fax +267 3696234 / email: contact@fsg.co.bw
Website: http://www.fsg.co.bw/thankyou.php
Plot 8448 Mica Way, Broadhurst,
GABORONE.
Tel (+267) 368 5711; Fax (+267) 3904912

Their services include:

1. Funeral insurance
2. Repatriation of mortal remains.
3. Cremation
4. 24hour mortuary facilities
5. Professional embalming

LESOTHO

AMPATH/MASERU NETCARE LAB

QUEEN MAMOHATO Memorial Hospital, Botsabelo, MASERU, Tel (051-400 0700)

MASERU Private Hospital depot. Ha Thetsane, MASERU. Tel (+266) 2231 0008

MOZAMBIQUE

Clinica de Sommerschield, 52 Rua Pereira Do Lago, MAPUTO. Tel (+258) 88 474 6441

NAMIBIA

Namibia Institute of Pathology offers medical laboratory services to both the public and private sectors in thirty seven sites all over Namibia. It is situated

At NIP Head Office, Katutura Hospital, Corner of Diedericht Street and Independence Avenue, Windhoek.
Tel (+264 61) 2954201

PathCare/Dietrich, Voigt, Mia & Partners, PathCare Business Centre, PathCare Park, Neels Bothma Street, N1 City, GOODWOOD, CAPE TOWN, 7460.
Tel (+27 21) 596 3400 or 596 2130 or 0860 100 442

SWAZILAND

The Clinic, MBABANE. Tel (+2687) 404 2368
Manzini Depot: 10 Bishop's Court, Sandlane Street, MANZINI.
Tel (+2687) 505 8209

ZIMBABWE

Lancet, 23 Fife Avenue, Corner Blakiston Street, HARARE.
Tel (+263) 470 6365 or (+263) 470 7142 or (+263) 479 2256 or (+263) 476 4423
Fax (+263) 425 0469

Bulawayo Hospital
Tel +263 9 212011

Victoria Falls Medical Centre
Tel +263 13 43356
(After hours number - +263 774 8559)

Victoria Falls Bridge (Customs and Immigration):
Tel +263 13 44238

Victoria Falls Police :
+263 13 42206

Chapter Seven

THE FAMILY ADVOCATE

In South Africa the office of the Family Advocate exists and operates under the auspices of the Department of Justice and Constitutional Development.

Duties of a Family Advocate

Offers assistance to feuding parties, commonly estranged parents of a child/children, where custody of, access to and guardian of such children is in dispute. It is common that one spouse elopes with a child/children to a foreign country whilst exercise his/her visitation rights (of access) to the child.

The Family Advocate will therefore evaluate each parties' circumstances-keeping in mind the best interests of the child/children in mind-and make recommendations to the relevant court with regards to custody, access and guardianship.

Such a service often comes in handy when:

1. Spouses are engaged in a "messy" divorce.
2. One party in a dispute applies for variation of a custody, guardianship or access order.
3. A customary marriage is dissolved and the feuding parties request definition of access, custody, access or guardianship.
4. An unwed father applies for custody, access or guardianship to his minor child/children.
5. The court specifically orders the Family Advocate to intervene in a matter involving minor or dependent children.

Access to the Family Advocate

Access to the Family Advocate can be had through direct access to his/her office or via a social worker or the local prosecutor's/magistrate's office. Once an application has been instituted, the Family Advocate will most often mobilise the services of a Family Counsellor (normally a trained Social Worker) who'll interview both parties to get detailed information about the case. The children in question will also be interviewed (in a non-threatening environment, in the absence of the parents wherever possible). This opportunity prevents the children from testifying in court.

Salient facts about the Family Advocate

1. The Family Advocate cannot be in a matter that has already been finalized in a court of law.
2. The Family Advocate cannot be subpoenaed to Court as a witness to give evidence on behalf of any party even if his/her recommendation is in favour of that party.
3. The recommendation of the Family Advocate is intended

to assist the Court in adjudicating a matter and arriving at a particular order. The recommendation itself is not enforceable unless incorporated in a Court Order.

4. The Family Advocate is a neutral institution and cannot act as the legal representative for either litigant in a matter.

Benefits of engaging the services of a Family Advocate are:

1. Reduction of costs and time if parties reach agreement on disputed issues-thus preventing the matter from proceeding to a Court trial.

2. Affords the child/children an opportunity to be heard in regard to their position in the parties' pending divorce.

3. Neutrality which focuses solely on the best interests of the child/children.

4. The environment in the Office of the Family Advocate is child-friendly, less formal than a court of law.

5. Usage of alternative dispute resolution techniques which are intended to reduce-if not eliminate acrimony between feuding parties.

6. Access to various Allied healthcare providers, for instance, Social Workers, Educational Psychologists, Psychiatrists, Speech Therapists, Physiotherapists and Occupational Therapists) to assist the family towards aiming for what's best for the child/children.

Chapter Eight

POLICE SERVICES IN COUNTRIES NEIGHBOURING SOUTH AFRICA

BOTSWANA

Botswana has a well organized police service spread out in fifteen police districts.

Toll free numbers
Mogoditshana   0800 600 107;
Broadhurst   0800 600 084;
CID Head Quarters   0800 600 125 or 999 for emergencies

LESOTHO

In Lesotho police services are run by the Lesotho Mounted Police Service with its headquarters in Maseru Police Station [29°18'47"-27°29'0'E].

Telephone: (+266) 22 323869.

It takes care of eleven districts-each with its own police station. These are Qacha's Neck, Maseru Rural, Thaba Tseka, Maseru Urban and police Headquarters, Berea, Mokhotlong, Butha Buthe, Leribe, Mohale's Hoek, Quthing and Mafeteng.

The local branch of Interpol is also headquartered within the precinct of Maseru Police Station.

Directions

From Maseru Sun Hotel-a stone's throw from Maseru Bridge Border post-head north-west on Orpen Road for 588 meters and then turn left into Mpilo Boulevard. Keep on this road for 138 meters and then turn right into Constitution Road along which you'll have to travel for 616 meters and then left and travel for only 64 meters to find your destination on the right.

From Maseru Bridge Border post head south-east on N8 for 2.8 kilometers and then turn left into Kingsway. Stay on this road for 1.5 kilometers and find your destination on the right.

MOZAMBIQUE

Police Services

Commando Geral:
Avenida Olof Palme, Maputo.
Tel (+25821) 320132/3/ Mobile: 823010688/9

Commando das Forcas de Intervencao Papida:
Avenida Olof Palme, Mozambique.
Tel (+25821) 400112.

Sala de Operacoes:
Avenida Ho Chi Min, Maputo Cidade.
Tel (Mobile) (+258) 826331808

Policia de Investigacao Criminal:
Rua John Issa, Maputo.
Tel (+25821) 305161 or 310502.

Posto Policial de Ressano Garcia:
Ressano Garcia border post.
Tel (+25821) 550126

Posto Policial da Ponto de Ouro:
Ponta de Ouro border post
Tel (+25821) 650074

Sala de Operacoes:
Xai Xai, GAZA Province. Xai Xai.
Tel (+25828) 225364.

Sala de Operacoes:
Inhambane Province: Inhambane.
Tel (+25829) 321375

Comando Da Forca de Intervencao Rapida:
Avenida Samora Machel, Inhambane.
Tel (+25829) 321311

Jails

Cadeia central de Maputo:
Rua do Jardim, Maputo.
(Tel (+25821) 706690 and 706945.

Cadeia da Machava:

Rua 4 de Outobro, Machava.
Tel (+25821) 706866

Posto de Controlo de Michafutene:
Estrada Nacional, Michafutene.
Tel (+25821) 759644.

Maputo Provincia Sala de Operacoes:
Avenida 25 de Setembro, Matola.
Tel (+25821) 782929 or 782966.

NAMIBIA

The Namibian Police (NAMPOL) is part of the Department of Home Affairs. Its head-an inspector general-is based at Lazarette Street)corner Independence Avenue , Auspannplatz.
Tel (+264) (2) 209 3111 or 061 230410.

Complaints Directorate is headed by Commissioner Ndelunga at the above address on Tel 061 220621; Fax 061 2093265. Deputy Commissioner Visser is accessible at the same telephone number and physical address.

Windhoek Central Police Station:
Telephone number is (+264) (0) 61 209 4339.

NAMPOL is an affiliate of INTERPOL. Other police stations in Namibia are:

Aus, Namib Naukluft.	Tel (+264) 63 25 8005
Bullspoort, Namib Naukluft.	Tel (+264) 63 69 3371
Dordabis, Central Namibia.	Tel (+264) 62 57 3514

Fransfontein, Khorixas Area, Damaraland. Tel (+264) 67 33 1823

Gobabis [22°45'S-19°00'E] police station is situated behind the Netherlands Reformed Church which is situated along Cuito Carnavale Street in Gobabis.

Hosea Kutako International Airport, Khomas.
Tel (+264) 61 2955600

Khorixas, Kunene, Damaraland.   Tel (+264) 67 33 1039
Maltahohe, Hardap, Central Namibia.   Tel (+264) 63 293005

Oshikoto Region- Police Head Quarters. Directions:
From Windhoek head north to Otjiwarongo and then north-east to Tsumeb). Head north and turn right into King Jafet Munkundi Street. Travel for 280 meters and then turn left into D 3626. Travel for 550 meters and then turn right into C41. Sixty nine later turn into C 46 and travel for 34, 6 kilometers through Ondangwa and then Okakwa.

Continue along B1 for 250 kilometers and then turn left into Pendukeni livula-litana Street. Take the second right turn and find your destination on the right.

Otjondeka Police Station, Kaokoland.   Tel (+264) 65 275102

Rehoboth, Hardap.   Tel (+264) 62 52 3223

Swakopmund, Skeleton Coast.   Tel (+264) 64 41 5000

Walvis Bay, Erongo, Skeleton Coast.   Tel (+264) 64 21 9048

Witvlei Police Station, Central Namibia. Tel (+264) 62 57 0002

SWAZILAND

The Royal Swaziland Police Service (RSPS) has its command control at the capital city of Mbabane. It is headed by a Commissioner who has two deputies and eight directors who head various departmental portfolios. Each of the four geographic regions (Hhohho, Manzini,Lubombo and Shiselweni) have regional headquarters and three, eight, seven and six police stations respectively. These regions' activities are supplemented by thirty two manned satellite police posts. All fifteen international border posts have dedicated police service posts.

Operational units

1. Dog Unit-responsible for investigating illicit drugs and related substances.
2. Domestic Violence, Sexual Offences and Child Protection Unit
3. Fraud and Commercial Crimes Unit
4. Organized Crime Unit
5. Serious Crimes Unit-which is represented in each police station and handles all type/forms of serious crimes.
6. Crime Prevention Unit-responsible for public sensitization, education and awareness on the perils of crime and fostering close working relations with community based policing forums.
7. Stock Theft Unit

The RSPS is affiliated to Interpol, International police Association (IPA) and the Southern African Region Police Chiefs Co-operation Organization (SARPCCO.

Emergency Contact numbers

For emergencies call (toll free):	999 or 9999
Child abuse/Domestic violence:	975 or 2404 6373
Public Relations Officer:	76062312 or 2404 3611 or 77800323

Email correspondence: rsppro@realnet.co.sz

GPS coordinates and phone numbers of various police stations in Swaziland [(Telephone code: +268) (7)]

Hlatikhulu	[2700S-3140E]	2176222
Lobamba	[2647S-3120E]	416 1221
Lomahasha	[2600S-3200E]	383 8810
Malkerns	[2645S-3125E]	528 3011
Manzini	[2630S-3138E]	505 2221
Mbabane	[2625S-3125E]	404 2221
Nhlangano	[2725S-3120E]	207 8222
Pigg's Peak	[2555S-3136E]	437 1222
Tshaneni	[2558S-3150E]	323 2074
Simunye	[2633S-3150E]	383 8966
Siteki	[2640S-3150E]	343 4222

ZIMBABWE

Zimbabwe Republic Police (ZRP) fall under the ministry of Home Affairs. Its head quarters are in the corner of Josiah Chinamano and Tenth Streets, Harare.
Tel 700-170/9 and fax 724-216

Other emergency numbers that can be dialled directly from a landline are:

Police:	(+263 4) 995 or 777-777
Ambulance:	994
Mobile Air Rescue Services (MARS):	727-540

Emergency Medical Rescue Ambulance Service: 250-011
                                            or 250-012
Fire Brigade: 993 or 783-983

(These numbers may be accessed by dialling 112 on am mobile phone.)
Beitbridge Police station: 0286-22552
Beitbridge Hospital: 0286-22571

All major towns have accessible police stations.

Harare Police Station telephone numbers

Police Central   (+263 4) 748836 or (+263 4) 77651
Police Avondale   (+263 4) 336632
Police Borrowdale   (+263 4) 860067 or (+263 4) 860061
Police Highlands   (+263 4) 495304 or (+263 4) 495504
Police Mabelreign   (+263 4) 336000
Police Milton Park   (+263 4) 799298 or (+263 4) 708113

The Director of Public Prosecutions:
Tel (+263 4) 774-586/7

Zimbabwe District Offices where community services
(including consular services) may be accessed are:

Bindura   +263 71 6511 or +263 71 6119
Bulawayo   +263 9 68491
Chinoyi   +263 67 23013
Gwanda   +263 84 22587 or +263 84 22618
Gweru   +263 54 223155
Harare   +263 4 702295
Masvingo   +263 39 263876 or +263 39 263705
Mutare   +263 20 60701 or +263 20 60276

INTERPOL IN SOUTHERN AFRICA

All countries neighbouring South Africa are Interpol members/ affiliates and accommodate Interpol personnel in their respective headquarters.

INTERPOL routinely publishes notices at the request of National Central Bureaus (NCBs) in any of its four official languages (Arabic, English, French and Spanish).

INTERPOL assists national police forces of member countries in identifying and locating persons wanted in those respective countries for a variety of offences.   The United Nations (UN), International Criminal Tribunals and the International Criminal Court use these notices to seek, identify and charge/prosecute persons who-within their jurisdiction-are suspected of or wanted for genocide, war crimes and crimes against humanity.

Types of Notices

- Red Notice – To seek the location and arrest of wanted person(s) with a view to extradition or similar lawful action.
- Blue Notice- To collect additional information about a person's identity, location, or activities in relation to a crime.
- Green Notice- To provide warnings and intelligence about persons who have committed criminal offences and are likely to repeat these crimes in other countries.
- Yellow Notice- To help locate missing persons, often minors, or to help identify persons who are unable to identify themselves.
- Black Notice- To seek information on unidentified bodies.
- Orange Notice- To warn of an event, a person, an object

or a process representing a serious and imminent threat to public safety.

- Purple Notice- To seek or provide information on modi operandi, objects, devices and concealment methods used by criminals.
- INTERPOL-United Nations Security Council Special Notice- Issued for groups and individuals who are the targets of UN Security Council Sanctions Committee.

Nota Bene

Any person/individual who is subject to an INTERPOL notice should be considered innocent until proven guilty.

Furthermore INTERPOL is recognized as an official channel for transmitting requests for provisional arrest in a number of bilateral and multilateral extradition treaties, including the European Convention on Extradition, the Economic Community of West African States (ECOWAS) Convention on Extradition and the United Nations Model Treaty on Extradition.

Diffusions

A diffusion is-though similar to a notice-a less formal request for cooperation/alert mechanism circulated by a NCB directly to member countries of their choice or to the entire INTERPOL membership and is simultaneously recorded as such in the INTERPOL's information system.

CHAPTER NINE

HANDLING ADVERSE AND UNFORSEEN CIRCUMSTANCES

_____

1 How to lodge a claim from your travel insurance policy
    1.1 General requirements
        1.1.1 Completed and signed claims forms (
        commonly downloadable from the insurer's
        website)
        1.1.2 Copies of airline tickets
        1.1.3 Your Policy Certificate
        1.1.4 Bank Verification/bank details (copy of
        a cancelled personal check/cheque or the top
        half of your bank statement). It serves the
        purpose of receiving your refund payment,
        commonly by EFT)
    1.2 Specific types of claims requirements and the
    requisite documents
        1.2.1 For Accident claims
            1.2.1.1 Police/Accident report
            1.2.1.2 Detailed medical report (from

the medical practitioner who treated you while on your trip)

1.2.1.3   Contact details of the said medical practitioner

1.2.1.4   Invoices/Receipts for expenses incurred during the process of treatment

1.2.2   For Illness claims

1.2.2.1   Diagnosis and detailed medical report (from the medical practitioner who treated you while on your trip)

1.2.2.2   Contact details of the said medical practitioner

1.2.2.3   Medical report from your home country/usual medical practitioner

1.2.2.4   Invoices/Receipts for expenses incurred during the process of treatment

1.2.3   For personal accident claims

1.2.3.1   Detailed medical report (from the last medical practitioner to treat you or the one who certified the client dead.

1.2.3.2   A copy of the death certificate which includes the cause of death

1.2.3.3   A copy of the inquest and post mortem reports

1.2.3.4   A police report if the death is due to a motor vehicle accident

1.2.4   Cancellation or curtailment of trip (NB. Contact your designated helpline BEFORE making alternative travel arrangements)

1.2.4.1   Proof of payment made for travel costs

1.2.4.2   Confirmation from travel agent, airline, hotel, tour operator, et cetera, that no refund is due or portion that is non-refundable

1.2.4.3   Proof of cancellation fees or penalties (where applicable)

1.2.4.4   Medical certificates and/or death certificate confirming the reason/necessity for you to cancel or curtail your trip

1.2.4.5   Proof of additional travel costs incurred in the event of the curtailment of trip

1.2.5   Lost baggage claims

1.2.5.1   A passenger/property irregularity report and baggage tags (proving that the baggage was indeed checked in)

1.2.5.2   A police report in the event of theft/loss

1.2.5.3   Any settlement advices from the airline

1.2.5.4   Quotes/receipts to replace/repair lost/stolen/damaged items

1.2.5.5   Proof of ownership of items that are being claimed for

1.2.5.6   Valuation certificates (in respect of jewellery claims)

1.2.6   Delayed baggage claims

1.2.6.1   A passenger/property irregularity report confirming the length of delay and baggage tags (as proof that the baggage was indeed checked in)

1.2.6.2   Receipts for essential items purchased

1.2.6.3   Delivery report from airline/courier (when the baggage is returned to the owner)

1.2.6.4 Details of any compensation received from the airline

1.2.7 Loss of personal money and documents
1.2.7.1 Police and/or passenger/ property irregularity report
1.2.7.2 Foreign exchange receipts
1.2.7.3 Receipts/invoices of costs incurred to replace travel documents

1.2.8 Travel/trip delay
1.2.8.1 A passenger/property irregularity report confirming the length and reason for the delay
1.2.8.2 Receipts for essential expenses incurred
1.2.8.3 Details of any compensation from the airline

1.2.9 Ticket upgrade
1.2.9.1 Report from the airline confirming the overbooking and/ or late arrival of incoming flight and non-availability of onward transportation within the waiting period.

1.2.10 Natural disaster
1.2.10.1 Report from the appropriate authority confirming the reason and nature of the disaster and how long it lasted
1.2.10.2 Receipts for essential expenses incurred

1.2.11 Missed departure
1.2.11.1 Receipts of the extra accommodation and travel costs incurred
1.2.11.2 Repairer's report if missed departure is due to mechanical breakdown of the vehicle in which you were

travelling..

1.2.12 Missed connecting flight/transport.

1.2.12.1 Report from the airline confirming that your incoming flight was late.

.2.12.2 Report from the airline confirming that you missed your onward connecting flight and that there was no alternative onward transportation available to you within 6 hours of your arrival.

1.2.12.3 Receipts for reasonable essential expenses incurred

1.2.13 Pet care/emergency

1.2.13.1 Invoices/Receipts from the veterinary surgeon who cared for your pet(s).

1.2.13.2 Veterinary report

1.2.14 Hijack and/or wrongful detention

1.2.14.1 Report from the appropriate authority confirming details of the Hijack/wrongful detention including the duration of the act(s)

1.2.15 Legal expenses and advice: For this aspect any contact with an attorney (plus a report)/embassy/humanitarian agency will greatly assist settlement of this type of claim. Urgent contact through relevant helpline is strongly advised.

CAUTION

Pay special attention to exclusions in such policies PRIOR to embarking on your trip!!!

Remember that travel insurance does not replace your medical aid cover!!!

2 How to report a lost/stolen passport whilst travelling abroad and how to apply for a replacement travel document. (Leave certified photocopies of ALL critical documents with a trusted contact in your home country!!)

2.1 Contact the nearest embassy/consulate for help.

2.2 Be ready to undergo a consular interview and fill in a new/replacement passport application.

2.3 If possible, report to the nearest police station and have an affidavit-over and above the incident report-prepared.

2.4 Duplicate copies of critical documents should be handed over to the nearest consular office soonest-in order to expedite the process and help you resume your travels with the utmost minimum delay.

2.5 When travelling as a group, one person in the group-not necessarily your compatriot-may play the role of an identifying witness, for instance, a tour guide or group leader.

Special circumstances

- Passports are issued over weekends only in life and death situations.

- If the consular official is in doubt about your bon fides, a limited (three months) may be issued.

- Issuance of the new passport will be free if there's indisputable proof that the applicant lost all disposable money together with the passport or the applicant is a victim of a disaster or sudden and unavoidable civil unrest.

3 How to transport remains of deceased persons back to country of origin

3.1 General requirements

- Death certificate indicating the cause of death.
- The deceased' passport.
- Affidavit by local funeral undertaker confirming whether the remains are embalmed or not. For unembalmed remains a formal statement by designated local personnel is needed, stating that the deceased did not die from a communicable disease.
- A transit permit issued by local health authorities at the port of embarkation/exit.

3.2 Special circumstances

- If the death was unnatural, for instance, as a result of a motor vehicle accident, a full police incident report is important. Further reports (as a result of investigations) are also crucial in cases where legal suits may ensue.
- Religious dictates, for instance, in the case of the Muslim faith, time is of essence. Burial has to occur at most within 24hours from the onset of death.
- Exhumation and reburial of remains involves the legal system of the burial area (city/province, et cetera). The local magistrate's and Home Affairs offices will facilitate this process. The cost of exhumation and reburial-facilitated by the local funeral director and religious official-will be borne by the applicant.

CHAPTER TEN

ACTIVITIES OF HUMANITARIAN ORGANIZATIONS

1. Amnesty International
2. Gift of the Givers Foundation
3. Human Rights International
4. International Federation of Red Cross and Red Crescent Societies
5. Medecins Sans Frontieres (MSF)/Doctors Without Borders
6. Transparency International
7. United Nations Children's Fund (UNICEF)
8. United Nations High Commissioner for Refugees (UNHCR)

Amnesty International (AI-SA)

Contact details:
10th Floor, Braamfontein Centre, 23 Jorissen Street, Braamfontein, Johannesburg.

Tel. (0027) 11 3395505
Fax (0027) 11 3395548
Email: info@amnesty.org.za
Twitter: @amnestyonline

AI-SA is a global movement with three million supporters and is active in over 150 countries where it wages campaigns to end grave human rights abuses. It is completely independent and is funded mainly by its members and public donations.

It puts pressure on governments, armed political groups, companies and intergovernmental bodies via:

- Publication and promotion of research findings (in WIRE magazine and on the internet)
- Public demonstrations
- Vigils
- Letter-writing campaigns
- Human rights education
- Awareness-raising concerts
- Direct lobbying
- Targeted appeals
- Email petitions and other online actions
- Partnerships with local campaign groups
- Community activities
- Cooperation with student groups

Gift of the Givers Foundation-GTOG

Head Office:
290 Prince Alfred Street, Pietermaritzburg.
Tel (0027) 33 3450163 or (0027) 33 345 0175
Mobile (+27) 82 8723811 or (+27) 83 600 1426
Fax (+27) 33 394 3780 or (+27) 33 342 7489

Toll free number: 0800 786 777 or 0800 786 786 (for counselling services)
Email: info@giftofthegivers.org/southafrica@giftofthegivers.org
NPO No: 032-031
PBO No: 930018993

Malawi – Blantyre branch
Plot Number CC 893 Off Masauko Chipembere Highway,
Maselema Light Industrial Area, Blantyre.
Tel +265 184 2287 or +265 184 2654
Mobile +265 8888 444 11
Fax +265 184 2782
Email: malawi@giftofthegivers.org

GOTG started off as a mobile feeding scheme in 2008, running a mobile soup kitchen for the poor in Berea (Johannesburg). It now runs seven feeding points. It also spearheaded a food parcel distribution programme in 2002, becoming a service provider for South Africa's Department of Social Development for whom it distributed R60 million rand's worth of food parcels in KawZulu-Natal and the Eastern Cape. Since then its activities have reached Malawi ("Feed the Nation Fund") and other African and Middle Eastern countries.

It now is a robust disaster response agency which provides life saving aid in the form of search and rescue teams, medical personnel, medical equipment, medical supplies, medicines, vaccines, anti-malarial medication, high energy and protein supplements, food and water to people in more than thirty five countries.

It has spawned and supports diverse human development through twenty one project categories which include bursaries, agricultural self sustainability, water provision, counselling and life skills services, entrepreneurship and job creation, establishment of primary healthcare clinics and medical support hospitals, winter warmth and supply of new clothing and shoes, sports development, feeding schemes, food parcel distribution, supply of household and personal hygiene packs, educational support and toy distribution, provision of housing, care of the physically and mentally challenged, orphans and the elderly.

Human Rights Watch

Contact details:
First floor, Wilds View, Isle of Houghton, Boundary Road (at Cas O'Gowrie) Parktown, South Africa.
Tel (+27) 11 484 2640
Fax (+27) 11 484 2641
Twitter: @hrw

This global organization vigilantly safeguards human rights worldwide.

International Federation of Red Cross and Red Crescent Societies (IFRC)

Contact details:
- 794 Church Street, Arcadia,
  Tel (+27) 12 430 7335 or 6 o7
- 44 Wierda Street Road West, Wierda Valley, SANDTON.
  Tel (+27) 303 9700
- 1166 Schoeman Street, Hatfield, 0083 PRETORIA. Tel (+27) 12 4312000; Fax (+27) 12 431 2006.
  Email: wndebele@redcross.org.za

This is the world's largest humanitarian organization with 187 member societies, a secretariat in Geneva and 60 delegations strategically located around the world. It carries out relief operations in times of natural or man made disasters as well as strengthening the capacities of its member national societies, for instance, the South African Red Cross Society. Field delegations assist and advise national societies with relief operations, development programmes and regional cooperation.

IFRC's spectrum of activities includes;

1. Development work in disaster-hit areas, for instance, the Haiti earthquake and the Mozambican floods.
2. Provision of first aid and emergency medical response and epidemic control and health promotion.
3. Assistance with local integration and sheltering of migrants (be they internal, economic, social or political migrants).
4. Disaster risk reduction alleviation.
5. Rebuilding homes, lives (uniting next of kin) and social cohesion.
6. Negotiating disaster law challenges which hinder emergency disaster response, human reconciliation and recovery.
7. Humanitarian logistics-acquisition and delivery of critical supplies and services.

Medecins Sans Frontieres (MSF)/Doctors Without Borders

Contact details:
Third floor, Orion Building, 49 Jorissen Street, Braamfontein, 2017. JOHANNESBURG.
Tel (+27) 11 403 4440 or 1, or 2
Fax (+27) 11 403 4443
Email: office-joburg@joburg.msf.org

MSF renders emergency medical care in poorly resourced countries (more than sixty countries, in fact) in peace times and in times of conflict, epidemics, natural disasters as well as for people who are deliberately or inadvertently excluded from basic/life saving medical care.

Transparency International

Contact details:
NGO House, Methodist House, 114 Rissik Street, Braamfontein, 2017. Johannesburg
Tel (+27) 11 403 7746 or (+27) 11 403 4966
Fax (+27) 11 403 4966

Chairperson: Mr Hassen Lorgat who is accessible on hlorgat@sangoco.org.za

Transparency International is a global organization which fights corruption. In 1995 it launched a Corruption Perception index which scores each country annually. Such scores often help many governments to take notice and act against corruption within their administrations. Such scores are informed by political and economic analysts' comments as well as those of business people and global experts.

Focus areas include:

- Reporting corruption
- Offering tools to fight corruption
- International conventions (to publicise global corruption levels, et cetera)
- Running integrity awards
- Doing research on corruption and publishing updated Anti-corruption guides

UNICEF

Contact details:
Sixth floor, Metro Park Building, 351 Schoeman Street, Pretoria, 0001.
Tel (+27) 12 354 8201

Fax (+27) 12 354 8293 or 4
Email: pretoria@unicef.org
Twitter: http://twitter.com/UNICEF SA
Facebook: http://www.facebookcom/UNICEFSouthAfrica

UNICEF is a global authority and a pivotal advocate for children. It influences various types of stakeholders and decision makers to maximise care and nurturing of children at grassroots level. Through publishing thoroughly researched documents, it serves as a worldwide resource of up to date information on health, education and protection of children.

Thus all its programmes help children with:

- Their survival and development;
- Access to education in child-friendly schools;
- Protection of orphans and vulnerable children;
- Protection of legal rights of children.

UNHCR

Contact details:
Eight floor, Metro Park Building
351 Schoeman Street,
Pretoria.
Tel (+27) 12 338 5301 or (+27) 12 354 8000
Fax (+27) 12 322 0216 or (+27) 12 322 0221
Email: unhcrsa@unhcr.ch

UNHCR is part of the United Nations General Assembly. Its existence dates back to 1951. Its work is humanitarian and non-political. It provides international protection to refugees, seeks durable solutions to their plight and helps them with material assistance. It helps with repatriation of refugees to their countries of origin or helps them attain asylum in host countries. Material assistance is provided in the form of food, shelter, medical care, education and other social needs.

WHO

Contact details:
351 Schoeman Street, Pretoria, 0001.
Tel (+27) 12 305 7700
Fax (+27) 12 7729
Email: whosouthafrica@za.afro.who.int

The WHO is global authority on health matters. It partners and guides respective governments and a variety of stakeholders on the delivery of healthcare through thoroughly researched and updated topics on all aspects of healthcare, for instance, child and maternal health, management of endemic/pandemic diseases, healthcare delivery to incarcerated persons as well as care of migrant communities.

Its publications often form the basis/pivot for various governmental health policy enactments and design of disease management protocols.

Indirectly, therefore, the WHO influences even the quality of healthcare worker training in those respective countries.

Question: What do you gain from knowing about the activities of humanitarian organizations?

Answer: To the business traveller you now know where to access which services were you to consider opening a branch of your global empire in countries neighbouring South Africa. In turn, this knowledge will help your organization to accurately calculate the cost of doing business in sub-Saharan Africa. It'll also help your organization standardize the level of benefits that will accrue to your future employees-whether they'll be local persons or expatriates from your home country. Such costs-if not catered for correctly-can impact your parent company's bottom line heavily.

To the leisure traveller (especially the adventure traveller) such information will come in handy when you need expert care at short notice.

Chapter Eleven

GPS COORDINATES FOR TOWNS ALONG EXIT ROUTES AS WELL AS TOWNS BEYOND SOUTH AFRICAN BORDERS WHERE CRITICAL SERVICES CAN BE ACCESSED

CONVENIENT EXIT ROUTES TO BOTSWANA

At least five entry points into Botswana are available. The three most convenient ones will be detailed here:

1. Entry through Ramatlabama from Mafikeng City [25° 51'49"S-25° 38' 47"E] leads to Lobatse town 53km away, and the capital city of Gaborone 93km further on.

2. Entry through Pioneer/Skilpad Gate Border post [25°15'S-25°45'E] from Gauteng through Zeerust [25°32'42.08"S-26°04'44.54"E]. This is the shortest route from Gauteng Province to Gaborone [24°50'S-25°55'E]-which is 73km from the border post.

3. Entry through Grobler's Bridge/Martin's Drift [22°45'S-27°50'E], about 100km from Mokopane along the N11 freeway. Once through the border the town of Palapye [22°45'S-27°15'E] is nearly 70km further on.

CONVENIENT EXIT ROUTES TO LESOTHO

Entry into this mountainous kingdom is convenient through three points, namely, Maseru Bridge, Van Rooyen's Gate and Telle Bridge. Two other entry points are detailed hereunder.

1. Entry through Maseru Bridge [29°17'52"S-27°27'09"E] is reached from the N1 and then the N8. The border post is an easy 15km the border post town of Ladybrand. The King Moshoeshoe International Airport is less than 30km away.

2. From N6 branch off into R26 and follow that route to Van Stadensrus 64km away. The entry point is 35km further on, just past Welbedacht Dam and Caledon Nature Reserve in Makhaleng Bridge [30°15'S-27°20'E].

3. Alternatively, from the N6 branch off into the R58 at Aliwal North [30°41'37"S-26°42'32"E]. Four kilometres before Lady Grey turn left, drive past Hesrchel and Sterkspruit on the R392 onto Telle Bridge 118km from the N6.From the border post Moyeni (Quthing) town offers a convenient refreshment stop 17km further on. Mohale's Hoek-60km further on-is a good alternative.

4. Maputsoe Bridge-90km from Senekal on the N5- is accessible past the convenient Rosendal town, halfway through on the R70. Entry will be through the town of Ficksburg [28°45'S-28°15'E].Once inside Lesotho, Teyateyaneng [29°15'S-27°50'E] makes a suitable stop over 44km due South and

halfway through to the capital city of Maseru [29°35'S-27°45'E].

5. From Harrismith on the N3 (from either Durban or Johannesburg), the historic town of Bethlehem is 92km away. From Bethlehem the R712 leads south into the popular town of Clarens 36km away. Equidistant from Clarens is Fouriesburg on the R711, from which the Caledonspoort border is reached less than 12km due South. From the border post the small town of Butha Buthe on the A1 freeway makes for a good stop–over on your way to Maseru.

CONVENIENT EXIT ROUTES TO MOZAMBIQUE

The most convenient entry into this country is the Ressano Garcia/ Lebombo border [25°25'S-31°45'E] post on the N4. The capital city of Maputo [25°55'S-32°55'97"E] (in the Maputu province) is a leisurely 90km along the N4 toll route. Turn left into the E1 freeway into the capital city. This route becomes Avenida 24 De Julho (24th of July Avenue), a major access route into all the city's amenities and crucial services. For instance, the Central de Maputo hospital is at the corner of Avenida Salvador Allende and Avenida Eduardo Mondlane (off Avenida 24 De Julho).

(The Ponta do Ouro [26°45'S-32°55'E] entry point into Mozambique-on the north-eastern corner of KwaZulu-Natal-is only accessible by high clearance four-wheel drive SUV's or 4X4s.)

CONVENIENT EXIT ROUTES TO NAMIBIA

Entry into Namibia is possible through is possible through two convenient entry points, namely:

1.   Vioolsdrif border post [28°45'S-17°40'E] is accessible from Cape Town along the N7 freeway in the Western Cape. Along the B1 Grunau is 141km away and is a good place to stop and refresh oneself. 167km further on Keetmanshoop [26°30'S-18°25'E] is a large town with all basic and critical services.

2.   From Upington along the N10, Nakop border post [28°20'S-20°10'E] is found 132km away. This route is scenic, with the awesome Augrabies Falls and Augrabies National Park on the left, just past Lutzputs. From this point onwards the B3 freeway leads to Karasburg 131km away. The B1 freeway is easily reached 51km further on at Grunau. These two towns offer good stopover amenities.

CONVENIENT EXIT ROUTES TO SWAZILAND

This mountainous kingdom is 70% surrounded by South Africa. Travellers across South Africa-Swaziland are therefore spoiled for choice. The four most convenient entry points into Swaziland are:

1.   Golela/Lavumisa border post [27° 30' S 32° 21' E] is 340km from Durban on the N2 freeway toll route. Several fuel/gas/petrol and refreshment stops are available and well-spaced along this route. At the border post-on the Swaziland side-there's a filling station and a refurbished curio shopping complex. Heading due north through the traffic circle, this route leads to Lomahasha/Namaacha border post [26°00'S-32°00'E] 168km further on. Beyond this border post a small town of Boane [26°10'S-32°40'E] offers a convenient stopover, 35km shy of Maputo city.

2.   For travellers from Johannesburg East the most direct entry is along the N17 toll route past Bethal which is 205km from Germiston. From this small town travellers have to decide

whether to continue along the N17 –past a convenient major stop over town of Ermelo [26°45'S-30°10'E]-and enter Swaziland through the Oshoek/Ngwenya border post [26°25'S-31°15'E] 115km further on. Mbabane [26°36'S-31°35'E], the capital city is a leisurely 25km past the famous Ngwenya glass factory shop and two royal residences. Alternatively, they may latch onto the N2 whereafter they can enter Swaziland at the Bothashoop/Emahlatini [26°50'S-31°55'E] border post-along the R543-after a refreshing stop at the historic town of Piet Retief [27°03'S-30°49'E]. In less than 65km/one hour they will reach the bustling industrial town of Manzini [26°45'S-31°43'E]. The University of Swaziland, the Roman Catholic Church's cathedral, St Theresa School, Raleigh Fitkin Memorial School multidisciplinary complex and the Matsapha International airport are situated in this town.

3. Travellers from the north and east of the Mpumalanga province can conveniently enter Swaziland at the Jeppe's Reef/Matsamo border post [25°45'S-31°40'E] 40km from the N4 toll freeway on the R570 route. The off ramp from the N4 into the R570 is found less than two km past Malelane town [25°40'S-31°50'E], which has a golf course, a sugar factory, a juice concentrate factory and a convenient entry (called Malelane gate) into Kruger National Park. Several fruit farms border the N4 freeway as are different SATOUR grade B&B lodges.

4. Travellers who find themselves at Ressano/Garcia border post [26°30'S-32°00'E] may access Swaziland by turning left into the R571. Mananga border post [25°55'S-31°50'E] is 61km away along this route. Tonga Hospital [25°50'S-31°55'E], which has a helipad, is 8km from NAAS village which is halfway along the R571.

Cautionaries!!!

- Beware of loitering and unattended cattle and goats along the last two route detailed above.
- R571 passes through NAAS town, a bustling village with no less than eight supermarkets right next to each other, including two BOXER, one Pick N Pay, one U-SAVE SHOPRITE retail stores!
- A SHELL filling station is plonked right at the major intersection along the R571, which has NO robots/traffic lights.
- Three major banks (ABSA, FIRST NATIONAL AND STANDARD and one small competitor bank (Capitec) have fairly busy branches abutting the same intersection!

CONVENIENT EXIT ROUTES TO ZIMBABWE

Entry into Zimbabwe by road from South Africa follows a direct route from Johannesburg/Pretoria on the N1 toll freeway to Beitbridge border post [22°25'S-30°05'E]-a high quality route with several convenient towns offering refreshments, clean rest rooms, namely, Bela Bela [25°50'S-28°15'E](about one hour from Pretoria), Modimolle (about thirty minutes further on, Mokopane (about one hour beyond Modimolle), and Polokwane [23°55'S-29°30'E](a major city and capital of the Limpopo Province, one hour beyond Mokopane). Musina town, two hours beyond Polokwane, is a stone's throw from the fast-developing border post town of Beit Bridge.

From Beit Bridge one has two choices to access basic but critical services. These are:

1. Travel north-east along the A4 freeway to the city of Gweru [19°28'W-29°49'E]. On this route towns that offer basic

amenities and suitable refreshment stops are Lutombe [22°4'60"S-30°8'60"E] 45km from Beit Bridge, Rutenga [30°53'S-21°25'E] 135km from Beit Bridge, Ngundu [20°05'S-30°50'E] 52km further on, Masvingo [20°05'S-20°09'E], a tourist centre of Zimbabwe East which is 95km from Ngundu. From there another 105km takes you to a small village of Mvuma where you have to turn left into the A17 freeway in order to access the major city of Gweru 83km further on.

2. Alternatively one can take the A6 freeway which is a 316km stretch to the major city of Bulawayo [20°11'S-28°35'E]. This city is blessed with at least seven memorial sites of significant historical importance. Along this route there are seven stopover towns of which West Nicholson [21°04'S-29°22'E] is the largest one and has two cave monuments, namely, the Cave of Hands and the Mchelu Cave National Monument.